SWING ERA

New York

SWING ERA
New York

The Jazz Photographs of Charles Peterson

W. ROYAL STOKES

Photographic preparation by Don Peterson

Foreword by Stanley Dance

Temple University Press
Philadelphia

Temple University Press, Philadelphia 19122
Copyright © 1994 by W. Royal Stokes and
    Don Peterson
All rights reserved
Published 1994
Printed in the United States of America

This book is printed on acid-free paper.

**Library of Congress
Cataloging-in-Publication Data**

Stokes, W. Royal.
    Swing era New York : the jazz photographs of
Charles Peterson; photographic preparation by Don
Peterson; foreword by Stanley Dance.
        p.   cm.
    Includes index.
    ISBN 1–56639–227–6
    1. Jazz musicians—New York (N.Y.)—Portraits.
I. Peterson,
Charles.   II. Peterson, Don, 1931–   .
III. Title.
ML87.S878   1994
781.65′09747′ 1022—dc20   94-10200

In memory of Charles Peterson
and of his friends, the musicians
who were captured in his photographs

CONTENTS

FOREWORD

When Timme Rosenkrantz and I got off the Queen Mary in February 1937, we expected to have a good time. Timme had been to New York from Denmark before, and he had raised my high hopes considerably on the way over, but what we experienced far surpassed our expectations.

The so-called Swing Era was reaching its apogee. In three weeks, for example, I heard the big bands of Duke Ellington, Count Basie, Jimmie Lunceford, Earl Hines, Chick Webb, Fletcher Henderson, Benny Goodman, Tommy Dorsey, Mal Hallett, Teddy Hill, Willie Bryant, Louis Armstrong, Fats Waller, Erskine Hawkins, and Lucky Millinder—and went home disappointed at not hearing those of Bob Crosby, Red Norvo, and Andy Kirk! But big bands were by no means the whole scene. I heard Billie Holiday both with Basie and at the Uptown House, where Artie Shaw sat in; Stuff Smith at the Onyx; Pete Brown's trio at the Brittwood; Joe Marsala's Chicago-ans and jam sessions at the Hickory House, and small groups and pianists in many other clubs such as the Black Cat in the Village.

The venues were as varied as they were numerous. The Goodman band played at the Pennsylvania Hotel and Tommy Dorsey's, with Bud Freeman and Dave Tough, at the Commodore. Stage shows with bands were becoming common at big movie houses, and Benny Goodman did a week at the Paramount that drew huge, excited crowds. The main ports of call, however, were the Savoy and Renaissance ballrooms, the Apollo Theatre, and the Cotton Club.

Shortage of sleep was inevitable, especially since during the day there were always recording sessions to attend. I was at that time a contributor to the bilingual French magazine, *Jazz Hot*. Helen Oakley, one of its American correspondents, was busily recording Ellington and other small groups led by musicians such as Frank Newton, Chu Berry, and Billy

Kyle for Irving Mills's Variety label. So there was always something to hear in the afternoons too!

In short, it was a wild time when jazz was enjoying the greatest genuine popularity it was ever to know. Charles Peterson's photographs capture the spirit of those days better than any others, and it is marvelous to see so many giants of jazz when they were young or in their prime, when they and their fans were overjoyed about the success jazz was experiencing.

I planned to return the following year, but first Munich and then World War II intervened. Although I managed to renew my acquaintance with Ellington and his men in Paris in 1939, it was 1946 before I returned to New York and found a jazz scene radically changed in tone and attitude.

STANLEY DANCE
Vista, California

ACKNOWLEDGMENTS

It was Charles Peterson himself who, several years before his death in 1976, first conceived the idea of compiling for publication a volume of his jazz photographs, but he did little more toward that end than pen a ten-page account of his life.

During the 1980s his son, Don Peterson, began to restore the more than 5,000 negatives that had been left to his care by his father. Marketing of a dozen or so prints for publication in record reissue packages also took place during this time, and some thought was given to organizing a representative body of the collection for publication in book form. But the idea did not take flight until Don, persuaded to do so by me, began to examine the entire collection with a view toward such a project.

The mass of photos cooperated rather nicely, falling into place in terms of either areas of New York, specific musical activity, or genre. Once the organizing principle of six chapters had been designed, I began ordering the individual photos within the several chapters, researching the historical and biographical background of the era and the musicians, and writing the text. The information regarding dates and locations of shoots that Don Peterson provided constitutes a significant element in the substratum of this book, and the prints that he has taken such masterful care in producing from the negatives are the volume's *raison d'être*.

Don and I want to thank a number of individuals whose commitment to the preservation of jazz history is worthy of the highest praise. Some helped identify musicians whose names Charles Peterson had neglected to record. Others supplied facts unknown to us or clarified situations that puzzled us. Extending such assistance were Daniel Abraham, Julianne Altieri, Ernie Anderson, Louie Bellucci, Ed Berger, Johnny Blowers, Ed Burke, Al Casey, Althea Casey, Doc Cheatham, Pam

Cohen, Helen Oakley Dance, Stanley Dance, Frank Driggs, Bob Friedlander, Milt Gabler, Johnny Glasel, Bill Goodall, John Harding, Haywood Henry, Milt Hinton, Mona Hinton, Max Kaminsky, Nat Kinnear, Jerry Kline, Charles Linton, Lawrence Lucie, Don Marquis, Alma Mathews, Emmett Mathews, Viola Monte, Dan Morgenstern, Red Norvo, Hank O'Neal, Ivan Rolle, Loren Schoenberg, Artie Shapiro, Joe Showler, Jack Sohmer, Charles Stier, Neale Stokes, Ralph Sutton, Al Vollmer, Laurel Watson, Joe Wilder, Dave Winstein, Laurie Wright, Theo Zwicky, and the National Center for Film and Video Preservation at the American Film Institute.

Our especial gratitude has been earned by Stanley Dance and Jack Sohmer for reading the manuscript and setting me straight on minor errors and misjudgments that would otherwise have made their unwelcome way into the final text. Any infelicities that remain are sadly my doing alone. (Readers wishing to provide missing IDs or challenge any in the text are urged to write me c/o Temple University Press, Broad and Oxford Streets, Philadelphia, Pennsylvania 19122.)

Much appreciated is the care taken by Temple University Press throughout the several stages of this project, from the enthusiastic acceptance of the project by Janet Francendese and David Bartlett to the final stages of the book's preparation for publication by Charles Ault and Bill Stavru.

Our greatest thanks go to our families, without whose patience and support this seemingly interminable project would never have seen the light of day.

INTRODUCTION

In the second half of the 1930s and the first two years of the 1940s Charles Peterson was given the opportunity to record a vital scene of American performing arts. Stanley Dance, one of the foremost authorities on the Swing Era, points out in his Foreword to this volume what was unique about the period that constituted photographer Peterson's floruit.

Born in 1900, Peterson took up the banjo while in high school in Crookston, Minnesota. A decade later, after attending Tulane, Wesleyan, Cal Tech, and the Universities of Minnesota and North Dakota, and playing in several college dance bands, Peterson found himself in New York hobnobbing with the likes of jazzmen Eddie Condon, Pee Wee Russell, and Bix Beiderbecke. Before long he had joined the band of Wingy Manone for a Rosemont Ballroom engagement. Other musical associations followed, culminating in Peterson's three years as banjoist and guitarist with Rudy Vallee and His Connecticut Yankees. With Vallee, Peterson appeared on the vaudeville stage, made many radio broad-

casts, was in two feature films and a number of movie shorts, and recorded more than 150 78 rpm sides.

It was during this time that Peterson's circle of acquaintances in the jazz world broadened; not only had he become house guitarist at Columbia Records, where he found himself sitting beside Miff Mole, Rube Bloom, and other jazz artists who supplemented their incomes with studio work, but he had also begun to frequent Harlem night spots to catch Louis Armstrong, Billie Holiday, Lonnie Johnson, and others.

With the birth of his and Virginia Peterson's first child, Don, in 1931 and soon after this the imminent departure of the Vallee band for months on the road with "George White's Scandals," Charles Peterson decided it was time to put aside his instruments and stay close to home. Long interested in photography and determined to pursue it as his next career, he sought the advice of Edward Steichen, who had shot the Vallee band for *Vanity Fair* magazine.

The eminent photographer urged Peterson to attend the Clarence White School, which offered not only hands-on instruction in the use of camera, darkroom, etc., but also classes on art history. Clearly, it was at this institution that Peterson acquired—along with the technical skills that later served him so well—the eye for composition and the feel for light and shadow that put his work beyond mere documentation and into the realm of great visual art.

Peterson's talents were such that, upon completing his studies, he was soon making a living shooting lingerie and Buick ads and free-lancing for the *Saturday Evening Post, Collier's, Time,* and other high circulation magazines. By the mid-1930s Peterson had reentered the jazz world by persuading *Town and Country* to run a photographic spread on jazz. The accompanying, rather colorful, essay by novelist Frank Norris was titled "Hot Combination." This was among the first articles on jazz to appear in a major general interest magazine. The seven Peterson photos—of Bunny Berigan, Jack Teagarden, Joe Marsala, Teddy Wilson, George Van Eps, Bob Haggart, and Ray Bauduc—that illustrated the spread were shot at various locations and offered a sort of, by his estimation, ideal band.

Before long Peterson had become the photographer of choice in jazz matters for general interest magazines and for music and entertainment magazines such as *down beat, Metronome,* and *Stage.* Many of the photographs in this book appeared in such formats. However, few of Peterson's photographs have seen publication since those days.

Clearly, the presentation of Charles Peterson's art to both the jazz community and the wider world of those interested in the graphic arts, aesthetics, and cultural and social history is long overdue. Peterson's rare combination of attributes arguably sets him apart from virtually all photographers of the jazz idiom, at the very least from those shooting the period during which he worked: he was of inherently artistic sensibility, he acquired via rigorous schooling the necessary technical skills, and he had both a deep love for the jazz idiom and an intimate knowledge of the musicians who were his subjects. It was the fusion of these factors that made his images creations of a high artistic order.

To explain Charles Peterson's relatively short period of activity as jazz photographer—1935–42 and several shoots in, respectively, 1945 and 1950–51—it must be made clear that he was something of a Renaissance Man and autodidact who enjoyed several careers, as well as extended periods during which he applied his native genius in areas other than photography. After all, for a half-dozen years before he took up photography he was a professional musician, and he returned to this pursuit as an avocation much later in life.

Among his other areas of expertise were his knowledge of deep sea sailing and celestial

(text continues on page 5)

Charles Peterson at work at Jimmy Ryan's, circa 1940. The camera is a Speed Graphic press camera 4 × 5 inch format, the style of camera with which most—90 percent or more—of Peterson's shooting was done. In the mid-1940s he changed to a Crown Graphic, continuing to use the same film size. His secondary camera was an early model Leica, a classic 35mm camera. In the late 1930s Peterson's Leica photos regularly appeared in the prestigious *Leica Annual*.

Note on the table the paper wrappers from flashbulbs. When son Don was in his early teens he frequently accompanied his father on jazz club shooting assignments. It was his job to hold the flash unit on its long extension cord, often waiting five or ten minutes on the bandstand until his father determined just the right moment to catch the action.

Helen Hockaday (later, O'Brian, then Decker) is on the left with cigarette. Her daughter (from the first of her four marriages), Jolie Douglas, is in the foreground.

To the right of Helen is Joe Rhodes (with eyes closed) and his wife Clarice (smiling). In 1940 Rhodes was arranger and bassist for the Paramount Theatre house band. (Photo by George A. Douglas.)

Louis Armstrong, Zutty Singleton, and Charles Peterson at Zutty's Harlem apartment, February 1942. (Peterson composed this scene and then had Commodore label producer Milt Gabler click the shutter.) The framed photo on the left is Gene Krupa. The photo on the right is Armstrong's 1925 recording group the Hot Five, with, from the left, banjoist Johnny St. Cyr, trombonist Kid Ory, Armstrong, clarinetist Johnny Dodds, and pianist Lil Hardin, Armstrong's second wife. Below is Louis Armstrong's Savoy Ballroom Seven, with Zutty on the far left and Louis second from the right. Regular members Earl Hines and saxophonist Don Redman did not make this early 1928 shoot. The others are, beginning second from the left, banjoist and vocalist Mancy Carr, clarinetist and tenor saxophonist Jimmie Strong, trombonist Fred Robinson, and pianist Gene Anderson.

Charles Peterson and Pee Wee Russell at a party given by *Time* magazine music critic Carl Balliet and his wife Rachael in their Lexington Avenue apartment on December 29, 1940. The Petersons lived across the hall from the Balliets from 1940–42. The party was in honor of Budapest-born violin virtuoso Joseph Szigeti, who came to the United States in 1926 and had become a naturalized American citizen. Szigeti was, along with Benny Goodman, a dedicatee of Béla Bartók's chamber music work "Contrasts for Clarinet, Violin and Piano," which Szigeti, Goodman, and Bartók had recorded a half-year before this evening. Joining Pee Wee in providing music for the guests were pianist Joe Bushkin and guitarist Eddie Condon. That afternoon Peterson had attended a Sunday jam session at the Village Vanguard, where he captured on film pianist Joe Sullivan, tenor saxophonist Lester Young, and others.

navigation, which he put into practice aboard the two-master Gloucester fishing schooner the *Oretha F. Spinney*—the very craft used in the 1937 film *Captains Courageous* as the *We're Here*. His long-time friend, the actor Sterling Hayden, had purchased the schooner from MGM in order to indulge his own passion for ocean sailing and invited Peterson to come along as navigator and shipboard carpenter. They plied the Caribbean from April 1942 into the fall of that year. Shortly after that, as a Boatswain's Mate First Class and again aboard a schooner, Peterson served for about a year with the Offshore Patrol of the U.S. Coast Guard on antisubmarine patrol.

As still other examples of Peterson's diverse talents, we note that he was employed as an ad copy writer, a real estate salesman, and an installer of fire escapes and other wrought iron fixtures. During World War II he built a tractor from used automobile parts for use on the 16-acre farm in eastern Pennsylvania where the family lived for a time. He was a professional-class blacksmith, machinist, and general mechanic. In his final years Peterson took up the precision building of live steam,

miniature locomotives. This activity was one of his pastimes while residing, for the last decade of his life, in the Chevy Chase, Maryland, home of his son Don Peterson.

Several years before he died from severe burns suffered in a fire that he set while smoking in bed, Peterson penned a several-page account of his life and careers. The penultimate paragraph reads, in part, "And so, Ladies and Gentlemen, that's how a fugitive from a Minnesota wheat farm became a banjo-guitar player [and] a photographer." Notwithstanding his numerous other self-taught skills, he here makes clear that his artistic urges were most fully realized with stringed instrument or camera in hand.

In addition to his son Don, who provided the essential materials that constitute the visual elements of this volume, jazz photographer *par excellence* Charles Peterson is survived by his former wife, Virginia Peterson Rees (the couple were divorced in 1966); his daughter, Karen Yochim; and four grandchildren, Carolyn Peterson, Randall Peterson, David Peterson, and Schascle (Twinkle) Huygens.

Sidney Bechet on the bandstand of the Mimo Club, 132nd Street, February 16, 1941. The New Orleans-born soprano saxophonist and clarinetist resided in Harlem in the 1930s and 1940s and several times led combos in this club. Bassist Wellman Braud, with Bechet for this engagement (right background), and pianist Cliff Jackson were among those who worked with him at the Mimo.

Duke Ellington said, "Of all the musicians Bechet to me was the very epitome of jazz. He represented and executed everything that had to do with the beauty of it all, and everything he played in his whole life was completely original. . . . He was truly a great man and no one has ever been able to play like him. He has his own ideas and nobody could execute the music from the same perspective, accomplish the same musical ends. . . . I honestly think he was the most unique man ever to be in this music."[1] For most of his final decade Sidney Bechet lived in France, where he became a national hero. He died there in 1959.

CHAPTER 1

Harlem

Harlem in the 1920s and 1930s was not simply a veritable city unto itself, it was the cultural center of African-American culture. The artistic and intellectual activity that transpired there during this era, known as the Harlem Renaissance, constitutes a heritage that stands up to that of any other period of American cultural history; indeed, it surpasses in riches many of them. The early history of jazz cannot be properly understood without due attention to this ferment of creativity, which exploded in Harlem at the conclusion of WW I and continued until the mid-1930s.

Far from being an isolated phenomenon, jazz was a part—a most important part—of this ferment. It inspired poetry, served as a backdrop in fiction, provided the pulse for dance and the orchestrations of musical theater, and supplied themes for the pictorial and plastic arts.

Some of the many great African-American creative artists and intellectuals active in Harlem or associated with the Harlem Renaissance during the seminal decade and a half that it flourished were poets Countee Cullen and Langston Hughes; novelist/editor Jessie Fauset; poet/novelist Claude McKay; playwright/novelist/short story writer Zora Neale Hurston; actress Rose McClendon; singers Ada ("Bricktop") Smith, Alberta Hunter, and Adelaide Hall; singer/dancers Florence Mills and Josephine Baker; singer/actress Ethel Waters; singer/actor Paul Robeson; dancer Bill ("Bojangles") Robinson; entertainer Bert Williams; conductor/composer Will Marion Cook; composer William Grant Still; painters Aaron Douglas and Romare Bearden; cartoonist E. Simms Campbell; sculptress Augusta Savage; photographer James Van Der Zee; educators/writers Sterling Brown and Alain Locke; and polymath W. E. B. Du Bois.[2]

It was really not until the Harlem Renaissance had faded that jazz "went downtown," as the parlance of the time put it. "I didn't know of much jazz being available in the New York area except in Harlem," said white multi-instrumentalist Spencer Clark, speaking of the 1920s and early 1930s. "You could walk into any of a dozen clubs in Harlem and hear some great jazz. . . . I didn't get to know them well enough to know from where they had come, but the guys were great to us. They let us sit in, said we should come there and make ourselves comfortable and at home. We learned a great deal with the boys up in Harlem 'cause they were all good players and they had that feeling, that wonderful feeling that we were groping for."[3] By the mid-1930s some black bands, big and small, had begun to appear at downtown Manhattan venues.

The other side of the coin was that the clubs, concert halls, ballrooms, and other venues downtown were for white patrons only, as indeed were a dozen or so of the plusher Harlem nightspots, including the Cotton Club and Connie's Inn. It was Barney Josephson, by opening in early 1938 the integrated Café Society Downtown, who took the first step toward breaking down the color barrier vis-à-vis jazz audiences in downtown New York.[4] But Harlem had been a nocturnal playground for nonresident whites since the 1920s. The roster of the famous who regularly enjoyed its entertainments and favors is long. A representative, albeit much abbreviated, list of the prominent whose tastes ran to "slumming" in Harlem would include Lady Mountbatten, Governor Al Smith, Mayors Jimmy Walker and Fiorello La Guardia, Mae West, Tallulah Bankhead, Jimmy Durante, Texas Guinan, Phil Harris, and Carl Van Vechten.

Among the many, many young white musicians besides Spencer Clark who frequently sampled Harlem's jazz offerings were Artie Shaw, Benny Goodman, Tommy and Jimmy Dorsey, Jack Teagarden, Bud Freeman, and Dave Tough. Of course, Charles Peterson, camera in hand, was also a ready visitor to Harlem, sometimes no doubt in the company of those cited or one of his myriad other musical acquaintances in the jazz world of the late 1930s and early 1940s.

Two aspects of this opening chapter must be clarified. First, those depicted in this chapter by no means constitute all of the many band and combo leaders, featured sidemen, vocalists, and pianists who played Harlem in the era covered by this volume. Second, some of the photos were not taken in Harlem and are included in this chapter simply to represent artists who were important to the Harlem jazz scene. Peterson didn't shoot *everyone*. He only managed to get onto film *almost* everyone on the New York jazz scene of his time. Finally, let it be clarified that the points made in this paragraph generally apply, *mutatis mutandis*, to the chapters that follow.

FATS WALLER

Fats Waller grew up in Harlem, where his father was a preacher at the Abyssinian Baptist Church. In 1919, at the age of 15 and with nearly a decade of piano study behind him, Fats became house organist of the Lincoln Theater, playing for silent movies and vaudeville acts. Before long he was a participant in the "cutting contests" at small cellar clubs like The Rock and Leroy's that were frequented by older Harlem stride pianists, including his mentor James P. Johnson. Count Basie would frequently drop by the Lincoln and receive hands-on instruction by Fats "about the stops and things like that, and the important things that made the organ different from the piano."[5] As a keyboard virtuoso and brilliant improviser, either solo or with a band, Fats by the mid-1920s was a mainstay of the Harlem jazz scene. A prolific composer and irreverent interpreter of Tin Pan Alley lyrics, Fats Waller was known and loved by the public at large for his outgoing personality and sheer ability to entertain. Unfortunately, he lived hard and died at the age of 39 in 1943.

Photographer Charles Peterson took advantage of a May 1937 Fats Waller engagement at Harlem's Apollo Theatre and followed him to work as Fats paused to chat with friends and put together a meal from several street vendors. (For this series of shots Peterson used his secondary camera, a Leica 35mm.)

Fats greets popular singer Jackie (later, as a comedienne, "Moms") Mabley at the stage entrance of the Apollo. The man in the tilted hat and open-collar shirt is Don Donaldson, arranger and second pianist for Fats' big band. To the left of Donaldson is comedian Pigmeat Markham, famous for his "Heah come de Judge" routine. In the 1930s Markham was perhaps the most frequent performer at the Apollo.

Outside the Apollo stage door, Fats apparently examines a piece of clothing or material that saxophonist, vocalist, and band member Emmett Mathews displays to him. Emmett's wife Alma Mathews looks on.

Backstage at the Apollo, Bobby Hackett cuts loose on cornet for guitarist Eddie Condon, photographer Charles Peterson (who had someone click the shutter for him after he had set up the shot), and Fats.

Jackie Mabley looks on from the right as Fats and Mabley's female companion horse around at the Apollo's stage door with Colonel Hubert Fauntleroy Julian, a Canadian-trained pilot and Harlem hero popularly known as "The Black Eagle." His exploits included parachuting into Harlem while playing a saxophone, briefly commanding Haile Selassie's three-craft air force, and nose-diving a hydroplane into Flushing Bay in an aborted departure for Ethiopia.

Fats turns serious vis-à-vis a point being made by pianist Willie the Lion Smith.

At a private party in August 1939, Duke Ellington and Cab Calloway have some fun jiving on guitar and at the piano to the amusement of onlookers (from left) gospel singer and guitarist Sister Rosetta Tharpe (whose guitar Duke strums), cornetist Rex Stewart, and singer Ivie Anderson. Trumpeter Max Kaminsky can be seen above Cab in the background. The testimony of photographer Peterson and promoter Ernie Anderson, who was also present at the session, indicates that the man to the left of Ivie was a jazz fan and connected, perhaps by family, with the French diplomatic corps.

Harlem

Drummer Chick Webb, clarinetist Artie Shaw, and Duke Ellington at a huge jam session on March 14, 1937, produced by Helen Oakley on Irving Mills' behalf to launch the Master and Variety record labels. Marshall Stearns, John Hammond, Milt Gabler (kneeling here), and others connected with the United Hot Clubs of America (UHCA) helped organize the event. The location is the Brunswick recording studio, and the guests include jazz critic Helen Oakley (in white dress behind Duke), tenor saxophonist Teddy McRae (to the right of her), reed and flute player George James (to the right of McRae), *Life* magazine editorial associate Alexander King (far right with camera), jazz historian Stanley Dance (rear center—British-born Dance and Toronto native Helen Oakley met during his three-week visit in the United States that year and would marry in 1947), bassist Bob Haggart (smiling in rear far right), Taft Hotel dance band leader George Hall (towering over Chick), and trumpeter and Chick Webb friend Manny Fox (slightly obscured by Shaw's right shoulder). A high point of this historic session was Ella Fitzgerald backed by Rex Stewart.

Chick Webb's Harlem Stompers, a consistent victor in the Savoy's "Battles of the Bands," played the ballroom regularly from the late 1920s until the drummer's death in 1939. The Ellington band held forth in Harlem's whites-only Cotton Club from 1927–31. Artie Shaw, upon arriving in New York in the early 1930s, struck up a friendship with pianist Willie the Lion Smith and sat in regularly with him at Pod's and Jerry's, a former all-night Harlem speakeasy popular with both uptown black and downtown white musicians.

Pianist, composer, and arranger Fletcher Henderson laid much of the foundation for big band jazz and his star-studded orchestra often played the Savoy. He and trombonist J. C. Higginbotham chat between sets at Café Society Downtown on March 30, 1941. Trombonist Sandy Williams is behind J. C.

Benny Carter, another major shaper of the big band style, was booked into the Savoy Ballroom off and on for months at a time from March 1939 until early 1941. Here he leads a fourteen-member band at Nick's in Greenwich Village for a five-week residency beginning January 28, 1941. A clue to his reed/brass multi-instrumental skills is the presence of a metal derby to the left of him and, to its lower right, the barely visible clarinet and trumpet mouthpieces. Trombonist Jimmy Archey is in the background below the standing trumpet player (Lincoln Mills or Tom Lindsay), and to the left of him is trombonist Joe Britton (behind saxophone). At the extreme left can be seen part of the face of trombonist Vic Dickenson. The tenor saxophonist at far left is Al Gibson and the one at far right is Ernie Powell. Bill White and Jim Johnson are the altoists.

A star soloist in a number of bands, an alumnus of the Fletcher Henderson band, and a major innovator, Roy Eldridge introduced his own big band to New York in the Savoy Ballroom in 1938 and the next year played the Apollo Theatre and the Golden Gate Ballroom. Here, blowing into a metal derby for some very special sounds, he leads at the Arcadia Ballroom at Broadway and West 53rd Street, July 1939. Franz Jackson is on tenor saxophone, Roy's brother Joe Eldridge on alto, Eli Robinson (behind Roy) on trombone, and Panama Francis (background) on drums. The seated woman at the far left is vocalist Laurel Watson and the mostly off-camera tenorist on the far right is Prince Robinson. The trumpeter behind Franz's saxophone and the bassist are unknown.

Active as a leader from 1919, clarinetist and saxophonist Fess Williams was a familiar presence at the Savoy and other New York ballrooms in the 1920s and 1930s. He was the father of Rudy Williams, saxophonist and clarinetist with Al Cooper's Savoy Sultans; bassist Charles Mingus was his nephew. Here Fess, a master showman, demonstrates that a partially dismantled instrument has musical potential. Photographer Peterson takes creative advantage of the moment for a striking chiaroscuro effect.

In addition to leading his own combos, Texas-born Hot Lips Page worked with Ma Rainey, Bennie Moten, Count Basie, Artie Shaw, Eddie Condon, Ethel Waters, and many others. His big bands played such Harlem venues as the Apollo, the Plantation Club, and the Golden Gate Ballroom. A powerful trumpeter and an earthy singer, Lips lent masterful expression to the blues. Here he and Sidney Bechet participate in an early 1940s jam session at Jimmy Ryan's.

The centerpiece here is Mezz Mezzrow. In his autobiography,[6] Mezz tells of coming up in Chicago in the 1920s and his subsequent years as a resident of Harlem. A self-declared "voluntary Negro," he married a black woman and fathered a son with her. Entering Riker's Island prison in 1941 on a conviction for peddling marijuana, Mezz insisted that he was "colored" so that he would be assigned to a cell in the prison's black section, where he had friends, including some musicians. Issued a draft card upon his 1942 release, Mezz noted with satisfaction that his race was designated "Negro."

A tireless advocate of New Orleans jazz and black musicians in general, especially Louis Armstrong and Sidney Bechet, Mezz led integrated bands in the 1930s and 1940s, organized recording sessions, and produced records on his own King Jazz label. In the 1950s he settled in France, where he died in 1972. In this photo, taken on October 21, 1938, in the Club El Rio in midtown Manhattan, Mezz is flanked by bandleader/trombone virtuoso Tommy Dorsey and George Wettling, whose long career included drumming for many big and small bands.

Harlem

Two Swing Era giants and major innovators, tenor saxophonists Lester Young, dubbed "The President" by Billie Holiday, and Coleman Hawkins, the first to create a role in jazz for the tenor, which he accomplished while with Fletcher Henderson in the 1920s. Young was in the Count Basie band for its 1937 New York premiere in the Roseland Ballroom and for subsequent Apollo Theatre and Savoy engagements. Hawkins took his big band into the Apollo and Savoy in 1939, 1940, and 1941.

Hawk's robust sound and authoritative knowledge of harmony made him the model for most tenorists of his generation and for some who followed him. Always receptive to new musical ideas, he displayed an open mind toward the changes that younger musicians were introducing in the 1940s and occasionally worked with some of them, including Dizzy Gillespie, Charlie Parker, Thelonious Monk, Max Roach, J. J. Johnson, Miles Davis, and Fats Navarro.

The lighter tone and more subtle swing that Prez introduced in the mid-1930s constituted a stepping stone into modern jazz. "Lester's contribution was so great," bebop tenorist Dexter Gordon said. "When he started recording with Basie . . . he had a seemingly very different—it *was* very different—and new concept of playing. . . . What he was doing was in direct contrast to what Coleman Hawkins was doing. . . . Like he was dancing with his music . . . [and] his harmonic approach was very colorful and tasty."[7]

Young is pictured at a Village Vanguard jam session on December 29, 1940; Hawkins at a like occasion at the Greenhaven Inn, Mamaroneck, New York, 1939.

Sidney Bechet (left) joins the Mimo Club's owner (second from right) and Bill "Bojangles" Robinson, part owner of the club, for a drink between sets, February 16, 1941. Robinson's consummate tap dancing technique first gained notice in the 1928 revue *Blackbirds*, his Broadway debut, in which he introduced his tour de force signature piece, the "Stair Dance."

FEMALE VOCALISTS

Female singers loomed large on the Harlem scene. They were an essential element in the big bands that traveled the road from coast to coast and whose itineraries included the Apollo, the Savoy Ballroom, and other Harlem theaters and nightspots.

Billie Holiday's impact upon the use of the voice in jazz is truly inestimable. No vocalist—in jazz or popular music—has escaped her influence and for many she has been the starting point. "My main influence, as far as singers go, the lady that I *loved*, that I feel most indebted to, is Billie Holiday," said Sheila Jordan.[8] With combos backing her, "Lady Day" (so named by Lester Young) worked in many Harlem clubs and she appeared with big bands at the Savoy and other ballrooms and at the Apollo Theatre. Here Billie is at a Commodore recording session at the Brunswick World Broadcasting studio, April 20, 1939. Tenor saxophonist Kenneth Hollon is at the left in the background.

A mainstay of the Duke Ellington band from 1931 until 1942, Ivie Anderson had previously worked with a number of leaders in her native California, with Earl Hines at Chicago's Grand Terrace, and had toured with several revues. Of her Ellington said, "She was really an extraordinary artist and an extraordinary person. . . . They still talk about Ivie, and every girl singer we've had since has had to try to prevail over the Ivie Anderson image."[9] The scene depicted is an August 1939 private party and jam session organized for a *Life* photo spread (which unfortunately never ran in the magazine), with Duke at the piano, Hot Lips Page, trumpet, Ivie, J. C. Higginbotham, trombone, and Cab Calloway. Standing in the background is the French jazz fan.

A brilliant scat singer of both Swing Era and be-bop sensibilities and an interpreter *par excellence* of the great American songbook of Irving Berlin, George Gershwin, Duke Ellington, Harold Arlen, Cole Porter, and others, Ella Fitzgerald got her first break with her 1938 recording of that bit of nonsense, "A-Tisket A-Tasket," with the Chick Webb band. She worked as a single from the early 1940s, eventually traveling the world concert and festival circuit well into the 1980s. Café Society Downtown or Uptown, July 19, 1951.

A dance craze took the country by storm around 1910 as ballroom dancing became a major form of recreation that lasted for more than three decades. Many of the black big bands, and some of the white ones, played the Savoy, which was dubbed "The Home of Happy Feet" and was open every night.

"In 1929 I was in George Washington High School . . . [and] every Friday night . . . we went up to the Savoy Ballroom and plunked down our thirty-five cents and had a plate of spaghetti for a quarter or something," singer/dancer Peter Dean *reminisced, "and we would hear the most incredible music in the world. . . . There were two bandstands . . . [and] every evening there were two bands. . . . We used to run into bands like Chick Webb, Vernon Andrade, Teddy Hill, and Willie Bryant. I even heard a battle of music [in 1937] with Chick Webb and Benny Goodman, and by God almighty, Chick Webb cut Benny's band! . . . There were very few bands that could cut Chick Webb because he knew how to play that room, and boy did he play!*

"There was nothing like that ballroom. It was a block long and the floor was a beautiful parquet all varnished and shellacked. . . . I'd grab one of those 'high yellahs,' as we called them in those days, gorgeous girls, and I learned how to lindy hop. On the backbeat that floor would go up and down. . . . Well, it was really pandemonium. . . . I just loved it and everybody else loved it."[10]

The Lucky Millinder band was on the bill at the Savoy Ballroom on the evening this sequence of photos was taken in 1942. From the left: Archie Johnson, trumpet; Sister Rosetta Tharpe, guitar and vocal; Millinder (standing).

A crowd gathers to observe a couple in a "break-away," during which the two dancers separate and execute creative movements on their own before returning to each other and continuing as a couple.

Note the "draped" zoot suit with its high waist and baggy pegged pants and nearly knee-length jacket—high fashion for Harlem jitterbugs of the time. Popular accessories included narrow belts and ties, yard-long key chains, padded shoulders, zippered pants cuffs, and wing-tipped shoes. The women favored billowed or short pleated skirts and brown, black, or maroon and white saddle shoes.

With the Millinder orchestra in the background, the floor is crowded with couples catching their breath on a slow number.

Front row of band, from left: Abe Bolar, bass; Trevor Bacon, guitar; Panama Francis, drums; singer/guitarist Sister Rosetta Tharpe (seated and peering over cymbal); Stafford "Pazuza" Simon, tenor saxophone; George James and Billy Bowen, alto saxophones; Millinder (back to camera); Ernest Purce, baritone saxophone. In the back row, Nelson Bryant is the second trumpeter from the lid of the piano and Archie Johnson, trumpet, is to the right of him. George Stevenson, Joe Britton, and Eddie Morant are the trombonists. Pianist Bill Doggett is off-camera, far left.

An athletic young man masters a split, which was de rigueur for both males and females aspiring to bravura class as Lindy Hoppers.

Not caught in execution by photographer Peterson were some of the more acrobatic "air steps," which typically entailed flips and the trajectory of the woman over the head of her partner. Some of these moves were similar to—and probably in part inspired by—the jujitsu throws that were being de-picted in popular film of that time, e.g., in the *Mr. Moto* series (the initial feature of which was released in 1937).

Mention should be made of the spirit of intense competition among many of these extroverts, as the combined efforts of dancers, band, and on-lookers worked the Savoy Ballroom up to fever pitch.

We perhaps see here the conclusion of one such action followed by a dramatic withdrawal from the dance floor.

"I used to go up to Harlem," Dick Wellstood said. *"There was a place called the Hollywood and Monday night was piano night and a lot of piano players used to go up there, especially Art Tatum. They used to kind of stage 'battles' up there."*[11] Dick listed others he heard in the 1940s at the Harlem establishments he frequented as a teenager keen on learning stride piano—James P. Johnson, Willie the Lion Smith, Willie Gant, Marlowe Morris, Donald Lambert, Gimpy Irvis, and The Beetle (Stephen Henderson). A fuller roster of prominent participants in these after-hours competitions would include, besides those pictured here, Eubie Blake, Luckey Roberts, Duke Ellington, Count Basie, Claude Hopkins, Cliff Jackson, Joe Turner, Corky Williams, Raymond "Lippy" Boyette, Paul Seminole, and Abba Labba (Richard McLean).

Willie the Lion gives a good description of cutting contests in his 1964 autobiography. *"Here's how these bashes worked: the Lion would pound the keys for a mess of choruses and then shout to the next in line, 'Well, all right, take it from there,' and each tickler would take his turn, trying to improve on the melody. There was actually more arguing going on between the listeners than there was jealousy between us. Hard cash was bet on the outcome and more than once they'd get ready to fight between them as to who had won. We would embroider the melodies with our own original ideas and try to develop patterns that had more originality than those played before us. Sometimes it was just a question as to who could think up the most patterns within a given tune. It was pure improvisation."*[12]

Art Tatum at Café Society Downtown, December 11, 1940. In the 1940s pianist Billy Taylor would accompany the nearly blind keyboard genius on visits to after-hours clubs. "When he finished work he liked to go and hang out a little bit and listen to other players and singers and just drink beer and have some fun," Billy recalled. "There were some sessions that took place at . . . the Hollywood Bar in Harlem. Every Monday piano players would start gathering about nine or ten o'clock. Tatum wouldn't show up until maybe about one or two in the morning and by the time he got there all the heavies would be shootin' their best shots. So after a while, after everybody had played, Tatum would get up and play and give everybody a master class on how it should be done."[13]

James P. Johnson, the "Dean" of Harlem stride pianists and mentor of Fats Waller, is joined by two New Orleans transplants to New York, Sidney Bechet, on soprano saxophone, and Pops Foster, in a 1940 jam session at the New School of Social Research.

"My way was to get a cigar clenched between my teeth, my derby tilted back, knees crossed, and my back arched at a sharp angle against the back of the chair," said Willie the Lion Smith, describing his demeanor at cutting contests. "I'd cuss at the keyboard and then caress it with endearing words; a pianist who growls, hums, and talks to the piano is a guy who is trying hard to create something for himself."[14]

Pianist, composer, raconteur, and decorated World War I veteran, William Henry Joseph Bona-parte Bertholoff Smith is seen here participating in a jam session at the Park Lane Hotel, February 17, 1939. Zutty Singleton is on drums.

Clarence Profit's prowess on the ivories was highly respected by Art Tatum, who enjoyed facing off with him. Profit and his regular trio members, Ben Brown on bass, and Jimmy Shirley on guitar, are seen here in performance at the New Yorker Hotel, March 1940.

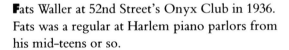
Fats Waller at 52nd Street's Onyx Club in 1936. Fats was a regular at Harlem piano parlors from his mid-teens or so.

Donald Lambert was active in his native New Jersey from the 1920s until his death in 1962. Notwithstanding his lack of fame, he was considered stiff competition for those stride "heavies" at the Harlem contests. Here dropping in on a December 15, 1940, Hot Record Society recording session of Jack Teagarden's Big Eight, "The Lamb" shows "Big T" what he can do.

LOUIS ARMSTRONG

Louis Armstrong had in the 1920s established the role of the soloist in jazz in both combos and big bands. In the 1930s he became an international star, fronting his own big band and frequently fitting in New York engagements at both downtown Manhattan establishments and Harlem venues.

The great virtuoso takes a solo in front of his orchestra at the Apollo Theatre in February 1942. From the left, Henderson Chambers, Norman Green, George Washington, trombones; Frank Galbreath, Gene Prince, Shelton "Scad" Hemphill, trumpets; Joe Garland, Rupert Cole, Carl B. Frye, Prince Robinson, saxophones; Big Sid Catlett, drums; Lawrence Lucie, guitar; Hayes Alvis, bass; Luis Russell, piano.

The popular Buck and Bubbles duo—pianist Buck Washington (here on washtub drums) and virtuoso tap dancer John Bubbles—are seen sharing a May 1937 bill with Louis Armstrong (and a movie) at the Paramount Theatre on Broadway. They were one of several acts (the Cab Calloway band was another) that "doubled" uptown and downtown, on the same day playing a morning and matinee schedule at the Apollo and several evening shows at the Paramount. Their popular act, which stayed together from the late teens for more than three decades, toured Europe in the 1930s.

Flit-gun at the ready in February 1942, Louis fumigates the room of the telltale fragrance. The pinched thumb and forefinger of the woman indicate that she holds the offending marijuana "roach." To the left of Armstrong is pianist Nick Aldridge, who appeared in the 1943 film "Stormy Weather" with a group billed as the Tramp Band.

The room is in the Braddock Hotel, which sat across the street from the Apollo's stage entrance and was a popular temporary residence for out-of-town performers at the theater. Photographer Peterson evidently shot from the left so that the mirror would not reflect the main impact of his flash.

At the table in drummer Zutty Singleton's Harlem apartment in February 1942, Charles Peterson, Louis, and his friend since their youthful New Orleans days have clearly enjoyed the host's chicken gumbo—as well as what Pops is pinching between thumb and index finger. Zutty appears to be showing Peterson how to hold a drumstick. As is always the case when he appears in the photo, photographer Peterson composed the frame and then had someone hold the camera and click the shutter, in this case Commodore record label producer Milt Gabler.

During the Apollo engagement the great trumpeter is visited in the Braddock by Lucille Wilson, who would later that year become his fourth, and final, wife.

First composing this late 1930s shot in his mind's eye, Charles Peterson created this montage of 52nd Street lights by continuing to expose the same frame of 35mm film until he had achieved the effect he wanted.

"The early Leicas were similar to modern 35mm cameras in that cocking the shutter automatically advanced the film to the next frame, thus preventing double exposures," Don Peterson explained. "To override this feature—and to make intentional *multiple exposures possible*—the photographer had the option of holding down the shutter release while reversing the speed dial until it clicked into place, thus keeping the same frame of film before the lens."[1]

CHAPTER 2

52nd Street

In the mid-1920s burgeoning development, concomitant increasing land values and rising taxes, changes in zoning regulations, and prohibition conspired to convert the block of New York's 52nd Street between Fifth and Sixth Avenues from a carriage trade residential area into a concentration of several dozen illegal drinking establishments. Entertainment of both questionable worth and great artistic value soon made its way into these mostly basement watering holes. After the repeal of the Twenty-third Amendment in early 1933, jazz gradually came to dominate as the featured offering at one club after another on "The Street."

Considering the musical action that enlivened this single block of brownstones during the 1930s and 1940s, it's no wonder Charles Peterson was able to capture the images of so many of the jazz artists of the era.

Tenor saxophonist Big Nick Nicholas said the clubs on 52nd Street "were like two or three feet from each other. . . . You could hear

Art Tatum here and go across the street and hear Billie Holiday. . . . Up the street was my idol, Coleman Hawkins."[2]

"Those were some very legendary days," vibraphonist Milt Jackson observed. "Just about everybody you could name . . . was right there, yeah . . . , every artist that was in the business and of any note whatsoever."[3]

Indeed, during the period that Charles Peterson plied his camera, hundreds of jazz performers worked the Onyx Club, The Famous Door, Kelly's Stable, the Yacht Club, the Hickory House, Jimmy Ryan's, the Three Deuces, and other 52nd Street venues that are the stuff of jazz history.

Charles and Virginia Peterson lived in an apartment above the Onyx Club for several years in the mid-1930s. Their son Don remembers being walked to kindergarten and passing by the jazz clubs that lined 52nd Street, an experience that did not mean much to him at the time because he was only vaguely aware that his father spent his evenings hanging out in one or another of these bistros.

Don recalls being occasionally dispossessed of his bedroom when his father brought back to the apartment one or another musician who was too far into his cups to make it home on his own. Prominent examples were Eddie Condon, Pee Wee Russell, and George Wettling.

Don has distinct memories of the frequent presence in the apartment of musicians such as Red Norvo, Mildred Bailey, Bud Freeman, and Bobby Hackett, who came to sample his father's liquor cabinet as well as his extensive record collection. Scotch, Debussy, Ravel, and "Rocky" Rachmaninoff were especial favorites.

The Spirits of Rhythm had become the house group of the Onyx Club shortly before its status changed from speakeasy to licensed establishment in early 1934. Leo Watson, the sextet's manic leader, vocalist, tipple player, and sometime drummer and trombonist, was always a draw at the club. Perhaps the most creative scat singer in jazz, he brought Harlem jive talk downtown and may have coined the word "zoot." This photo shows him at the Onyx during a return engagement in 1938.

Brass-playing singers and cut-ups Ed Farley and Mike Riley had a major record hit with their (and Red Hodgson's) song "The Music Goes 'Round and Around," which won a featured spot for the band in the film of the same title. Their pie-throwing and seltzer water–squirting antics drew crowds to the Onyx but turned off more dedicated musicians like guitarist Eddie Condon, who was fired when he refused to play with them. Here they are beneath their logo at the club in February 1936. The instrument Riley holds is most likely a Conn marching trombone.

In entertainment terms, Riley and Farley was a hard act to follow. The solution the club's owner Joe Helbock conceived was the Onyx debut of Stuff Smith's sextet. Of unorthodox instrumental technique and a furiously swinging improviser, violinist and singer Stuff was booked into the Onyx in 1936 and packed the club for months. From left: bassist Mack Walker, guitarist Bobby Bennett, pianist Clyde Hart, Stuff, trumpeter Jonah Jones, and drummer Cozy Cole at the Onyx on some date between March 3 and 14, 1937.

The mural of great luminaries of 1930s show business contains several recognizable individuals. Those standing on the side wall are, from the left, Greta Garbo, Merle Oberon, and Bette Davis. Kate Smith is at the bottom to the left of the piano. On the back wall are Lou Costello (above Hart) and Bud Abbott (above Jonah), who had been headliners as a vaudeville act since the early 1930s, and perhaps Ethel Merman (between Jonah and Cozy), who had been starring in films since 1930.

Peterson splendidly captured the showmanship of Stuff Smith and Jonah Jones in this publicity shot.

Jonah Jones, backed by Cozy Cole, takes a solo on opening night at the Onyx, April 14, 1938. The mounted photo to the right of Cozy is of Artie Shaw, taken at the Imperial Swing Concert of 1936 by Charles Peterson.

Guitarist Carl Kress, who would soon become the owner of the Onyx, sits in with the group on the same date. Stuff and Hot Lips Page flank bassist Wellman Braud, a first-generation jazz musician and alumnus of the Ellington band whose six-decade career included stays in New Orleans, Chicago, New York, the West Coast, and Europe. Zutty Singleton (mostly off-camera at right) is on drums. Seated at far left is singer Mildred Bailey. In the audience with backs to camera are regular band members Jonah Jones (beneath Lips), probably Clyde Hart, and bassist Mack Walker or John Brown. John Kirby is at far right in profile.

A former Fletcher Henderson band member, bassist John Kirby became leader of a sextet (soon dubbed "The Biggest Little Band") that became widely known for its subdued approach, tight arrangements, and gentle swing. Here in 1937 for one of the band's extended stays at the Onyx are guitarist Teddy Bunn, pianist Don Frye, Kirby, Leo Watson (behind drums with trombone), alto saxophonist Pete Brown, trumpeter Frankie Newton, and clarinetist Buster Bailey. The enlarged photo of the Stuff Smith group in the background was shot on the same bandstand by Charles Peterson.

Kirby and a muted Charlie Shavers, who replaced Newton in late 1937 and wrote many of the arrangements that made the sextet so distinctive, at the Onyx, April 7, 1939.

The horizontal white line in this stunning 1937 publicity photo of Maxine Sullivan by Charles Peterson is not a flaw—she is holding a thread that has unraveled from her jacket!

Maxine's 1937 recording of "Loch Lomond," arranged by bandleader Claude Thornhill, garnered her a profile in *The New Yorker* and she went on to a long, if intermittent, career that included extended engagements at New York clubs, recordings, a radio series with John Kirby (to whom she was married from 1938 to '41), several Hollywood and Broadway roles, and associations with Louis Armstrong, Benny Carter, Fats Waller, Benny Goodman, Bobby Hackett, Bob Wilber, Dick Hyman, and the World's Greatest Jazz Band.

Maxine Sullivan at the Onyx, October 20, 1938.
On the left are French jazz critic Hugues Panassié,
drummer O'Neil Spencer, and saxophonist Russell Procope. Buster Bailey accompanies.

Clarinetist Joe Marsala, leader here, and guitarist Eddie Condon, both of Chicago backgrounds, were among the first to organize integrated groups, as this 1936 presence of trumpeter Henry "Red" Allen verifies. Joe Bushkin is at the piano, Morty Stuhlmaker on bass. The location is the Hickory House, where Marsala would maintain extended residencies for more than a decade. The club also became known over the years for the piano talent it regularly featured, including, in addition to Bushkin, Mary Lou Williams, Billy Kyle, Mel Powell, Jess Stacy, Hazel Scott, Marian McPartland, Billy Taylor, Martial Solal, Jutta Hipp, and Toshiko Akiyoshi.

In January 1938 Lionel Hampton, here wielding four sticks, sat in at the Hickory House with a Joe Marsala band of somewhat different personnel. The leader's brother Marty (next to Hampton) is on trumpet as are also, for this number, pianist Joe Bushkin and guitarist-violinist Ray Biondi, both of whom doubled on the instrument. The bassist is Artie Shapiro and the leader holds forth on clarinet to the right. Not shown are harpist Adele Girard, who had married Marsala in 1937 and was a regular member of the band, and drummer Buddy Rich, whose drums Hamp gives a workout. The eight months spent with Marsala's band was twenty-year old Rich's first steady jazz gig.

Another leader who played the Hickory House, caught here at the club on July 21, 1938, was crowd-pleasing trumpeter/singer Wingy Manone, who as a child in New Orleans lost part of his right arm (from above the elbow) in a streetcar accident. Wingy may have, on this occasion, been sitting in with the combo that was temporarily replacing the house band of an ailing Joe Marsala. The trombonist is unknown.

Red Norvo introduced mallet instruments to jazz in the 1920s, at first playing marimba, then xylophone, and finally switching to the vibraphone in the early 1940s. A visionary who led both combos and big bands, Red made some recordings in 1933 with Benny Goodman on bass clarinet that anticipated some of the harmonic and rhythmic innova-tions of the 1950s "cool school." His Swing Sextet performs here in February 1936 at The Famous Door. Herbie Haymer is on tenor; Pete Peterson (no relation to the photographer), bass; Dave Barbour, guitar; Don McCook, clarinet; Stew Pletcher; trumpet.

Teddy Wilson was one of several intermission pianists at The Famous Door in the mid-1930s. This photo was taken in 1936.

Wilson sat in with Benny Goodman at a party at Red Norvo's house in 1935 and in the spring of 1936 joined the clarinetist's trio, an association that constituted a social and cultural watershed in that he was the first black to go on the road with a major white orchestra. He had previously worked in the big bands of Louis Armstrong and Benny Carter and would go on to lead his own combos and accompany Billie Holiday on many of her recordings.

Guitarist Eddie Condon (center background), another who played "The Door," was on this occasion in early 1936 co-leader with singer and tissue-wrapped comb player Red McKenzie (holding microphone). The group featured the extraordinarily talented trumpeter Bunny Berigan. Forrest Crawford is the tenor saxophonist, Morty Stuhlmaker is on bass, and Joe Bushkin is on piano.

Fats Waller took his small band into The Famous Door in 1939 but here he is on October 21, 1938, during a long engagement at the Yacht Club. It is said that upon catching sight of Art Tatum in the audience one night, Fats exclaimed, "I just play the piano. But God is in the house tonight!" The respect was reciprocal, for Tatum openly acknowledged Fats as his primary influence. Smiling above the pianist is French jazz critic Hugues Panassié.

Jimmy Ryan's club, which opened in 1940 at 53 West 52nd Street and relocated a couple of blocks away on 54th in 1962, was for more than four decades a bastion of traditional jazz. Here, at a Sunday jam session on January 19, 1941, are Brad Gowans, on valve trombone; cornetist Bobby Hackett, much admired for his pretty tone and lyrical expression; and the brilliant clarinetist Pee Wee Russell, whose idiosyncratic delivery and totally personal conception made him truly *sui generis*.

Drummer Jo Jones, a charter member of Count Basie's "All-American Rhythm Section" from 1935 until 1948 (with brief absences and time out for army service), at a jam session at Jimmy Ryan's on November 9, 1941. "Papa Jo," who had come up in carnival and territory bands, was the greatest Swing Era big band drummer, widely respected by drummers of his own and succeeding generations, and much in demand as a free-lancer throughout his long career. In addition to playing with Basie, Jones drummed for, or recorded with, Lionel Hampton, Benny Goodman, Duke Ellington, Harry James, Billie Holiday, Jazz at the Philharmonic, and others.

At the same session was Sandy Williams, whose most important association was with Chick Webb (1933–39). His trombone was also a mighty presence in the bands of Claude Hopkins, Fletcher Henderson, Duke Ellington, Lucky Millinder, Benny Carter, and Coleman Hawkins, as well as the combos of Wild Bill Davison, Rex Stewart, Art Hodes, Sidney Bechet, and others.

A grand old man of jazz, Pops Foster was born on a Louisiana sugar cane plantation in 1892. He came to New Orleans when he was ten years old, then settled in New York in 1929. His more than six-decade career included associations with King Oliver, Kid Ory, Louis Armstrong, Sidney Bechet, Earl Hines, Bob Wilber, and countless others. Pops is shown here at Jimmy Ryan's with trombonist Jimmy Archey's band. Behind Pops is reed-player Benny Waters, the replacement for Wilber, who had led the band the year before and then gone on to other pursuits. Born in 1902 and having played with King Oliver, Clarence Williams, and many others of the classic period of jazz, Waters was still professionally active into the 1990s. The other band members were trumpeter Henry Goodwin, pianist Dick Wellstood, and drummer Tommy Benford.

At 110 52nd Street, the Pic-A-Rib, which closed at 5 A.M., an hour later than the clubs, was an eatery and watering hole popular with musicians. Benny Goodman's brother, bassist Harry Goodman, was a part owner. In January 1939 Benny Goodman band pianist Jess Stacy converses, over Jack Teagarden's head, with the trombonist's third wife Billie Coates while drummer George Wettling digs into some ribs. At the far left is Virginia Peterson, wife of our photographer.

Harry Goodman hovers over bandleader Jimmy Dorsey (middle) as the pioneer jazz violinist and infamous prankster Joe Venuti reaches for Jimmy's rib. Music publisher Jack Bregman, apparently displaying it for the camera, holds the score of a Gus Kahn–Harry Warren song Jimmy's brother Tommy would record a few weeks hence.

The Greenhaven Inn, on Route 1 a few miles north of New York in Mamaroneck, attracted many prominent musicians to its jam sessions. On one of the Sundays between November 24 and December 14, 1939, the line-up was Hot Lips Page, trumpet; Coleman Hawkins, tenor saxophone; Joe Marsala, clarinet; Artie Shapiro, bass; and (above Hawk's left shoulder) Willie the Lion Smith, piano. Not shown is drummer George Wettling.

CHAPTER 3

Nick's, the Village Vanguard, Café Society, and Other Venues

To view the jazz scene in New York as having been confined to Harlem and 52nd Street would be tantamount to a claim that early-century British intellectual effort blossomed only in the Bloomsbury section of London. Yes, jazz activity was certainly heavily concentrated in those two locations, but it was scattered throughout the rest of the city as well and even found itself established here and there in the environs of Manhattan.

Charles Peterson did not overlook such promising photo opportunities as Nick's in Greenwich Village, downtown hotels, Carnegie Hall and other concert venues, the many clubs that resided on streets other than 52nd, and the odd habitat of jazz away from the Big Apple. He got around, as they say, and the photos that follow are the proof of that.

Nick's, the Village Vanguard, Café Society, and Other Venues

As a speakeasy from 1922 and then as a legal club with the repeal of Prohibition in 1933, Nick's Tavern had occupied several sites in the Village. In 1937 owner Nick Rongetti settled in at 10th Street and 7th Avenue and there the restaurant remained for the rest of its existence (until 1963) a major venue for traditional-style musicians and their younger disciples. In fact, the stylistic character of the music featured there was so well established that it became known as "Nicksieland."

The two groups pictured here on December 19, 1937, opened the new club and alternated sets for a few weeks until New Orleans trumpeter Sharkey Bonano's group (on the right) departed. The survivors (on the left) were nominally under the leadership of Bobby Hackett (with cornet on knee). Pee Wee Russell (with clarinet across thighs) is to the left of Bobby, and seated on the edge of the bandstand to the left of him is bassist Clyde Newcombe. Trombonist Georg Brunis is behind Pee Wee, and pianist Dave Bowman is to the left of him. Drummer Johnny Blowers stands at the rear left, and Red McKenzie (who organized the band) drapes his arm over Eddie Condon's shoulder.

On the right, Sharkey Bonano holds trumpet and Russ Papalia is the trombonist. Above Sharkey in the middle row is pianist Roy Zimmerman (left) and drummer Johnny Castaing. Clarinetist Bill Bourgeois is on the right in the top row.

Stephen Smith, a New York record store owner and co-producer of the Hot Record Society (HRS) label, chats at Nick's bar with Bobby Hackett (center) and Sharkey Bonano between sets on the same night.

Nick's, the Village Vanguard, Café Society, and Other Venues

A year later, December 1938, found some of the same players at Nick's but in a cooperative band dubbed Bud Freeman's Summa Cum Laude Orchestra. From the left: Dave Bowman, Eddie Condon, Pee Wee Russell, Stan King (who, since he is wearing a different color suit, was perhaps subbing for an ailing Dave Tough, absent from the drum set in foreground), trumpeter Max Kaminsky, bassist Clyde Newcombe, tenorist Bud Freeman, and valve trombonist Brad Gowans.

Others who performed at Nick's into the early 1940s were Sidney Bechet, clarinetist Albert Nicholas, Zutty Singleton, pianists James P. Johnson and Meade Lux Lewis, cornetists Wild Bill Davison and Muggsy Spanier, and the Spirits of Rhythm.

"Never had a night gone by that some world famous person did not come in to hear the band," Bud Freeman recalled, and went on to name John Steinbeck, Spencer Tracy, Joe DiMaggio, Willem de Kooning, Tallulah Bankhead, Peter Arno, Igor Stravinsky, and bank robber Willie Sutton as regular patrons of Nick's.[1]

Benny Carter at Nick's, where a January 1941 one-night stand was extended for a five-week residency for his big band. Multi-instrumentalist Carter lets his alto hang by its strap and takes a turn on trumpet. Of Carter's trumpet skills Dizzy Gillespie said, "He used to pick up his horn and play solos and wash out the trumpet players, man. He was always the best trumpet player in his band."[2] On the far right is tenor saxophonist Ernie Powell.

In the fall of 1938 the French jazz critic Hugues Panassié, on his first visit to the United States, came to New York to produce some record sessions for RCA Victor. In the course of seeking out musicians for his project he visited a number of clubs. In one of the longest shooting sessions of his career, photographer Peterson escorted Panassié from club to club for two long evenings, October 20th and 21st. Here, on the 21st, Panassié has been taken to lunch at Club El Rio on East 58th Street by Paul Whiteman. Panassié (wearing the bow tie) sits at the table with the orchestra leader. Whiteman's huge orchestra, loaded with prominent jazz musicians as featured soloists, then employed two on the bandstand here, trombonist Jack Teagarden (center) and pianist Frank Signorelli. The drummer is George Wettling, who would join Whiteman in December. Mezz Mezzrow is on clarinet; former Whiteman band trombonist Tommy Dorsey is on the far right.

Panassié also caught the quartet of Sidney Bechet, here on soprano saxophone, at Nick's on October 20th. Zutty Singleton is on drums.

Benny Carter, clarinet, and Hot Lips Page on muted trumpet provide accompaniment for Lee Wiley's vocal in Panassié's hotel room. Madeleine Gautier, poet, jazz critic, and colleague and traveling companion of Panassié, is on the right of Lips, peering over his shoulder.

Pee Wee Russell was fronting a quartet at the Little Club and Panassié dropped by on the 21st to catch the combo in rehearsal, perhaps in some hotel's somewhat seedy back room. Max Kaminsky is on trumpet, George Troup on trombone. Drummer Johnny Morris (left) and reed player Johnny Mince stand in the background and pianist Art Hodes stands at the right rear.

Several years before World War II, the blues piano style of boogie woogie surfaced from the bars and rent parties of the black sections of such urban centers as Chicago, Kansas City, and St. Louis and became ensconced in Café Society Downtown, at Sheridan Square, in the persons of Chicagoans Albert Ammons and Meade Lux Lewis, shown here. Also on the bill for the club opening in early 1939 were pianist Pete Johnson and blues singer Joe Turner, both out of Kansas City.

John Hammond, whose role as impresario was pivotal vis-à-vis the careers of many jazz, folk, and popular music artists from the 1930s to the 1980s, virtually singlehandedly introduced boogie woogie to a national audience by plucking Ammons, Johnson, and Lewis from obscurity and bringing them to New York. The genre's subsequent wide acceptance, popularized by big band orchestrations like Tommy Dorsey's "Boogie Woogie" (based on "Pinetop's Boogie Woogie," a 1928 recording by Pinetop Smith), amounted to a nationwide craze from the late 1930s through the mid-1940s.

Lena Horne (caught here as she visited backstage at Carnegie Hall during a concert of the Duke Ellington band in 1951) was among the many vocalists who appeared at Café Society Downtown and, when it opened the next year on East 58th Street, Café Society Uptown. Others were Billie Holiday, Ida Cox, Mildred Bailey, Josh White, Sarah Vaughan, Carol Channing, the Golden Gate Quartet, and the jazz-oriented, self-accompanying gospel singer Sister Rosetta Tharpe.

The woman to the right of Lena in this photo is Rachael Reis, the remarried widow of Carl Balliet, who had been music critic for *Time* magazine in the 1930s and 1940s.

Sister Rosetta Tharpe at Café Society Downtown on December 11, 1940. The pianist is Kenny Kersey and Jimmy Hoskins is on drums. Both were in Red Allen's band, which was also performing at the club that night, as was pianist Art Tatum.

Café Society Downtown and Café Society Uptown, it should be noted, had integrated audiences because the owner Barney Josephson wanted his clubs to be places "where blacks and whites worked together behind the footlights and sat together out front."[3]

Pianist Fletcher Henderson several times put together reunion performances from members of his
great bands of the 1920s and 1930s. Here is one
such gathering on March 30, 1941, at Café Society
Downtown. From the left: trombonist J. C. Higginbotham; clarinetist Buster Bailey; trombonist

Sandy Williams (behind Bailey); Henderson;
drummer Big Sid Catlett; bassist John Kirby;
trumpeter Henry "Red" Allen; saxophonists
Benny Carter and Russell Procope; and guitarist
Lawrence Lucie, who is mostly obscured by
Carter.

On the same date, Carter, Procope, and Bailey seem to be riffing beneath Allen's solo. Catlett, Kirby, and Lucie are in the background.

A New Orleans native and member of a prominent musical family, trumpeter Henry "Red" Allen settled in New York in the late 1920s and continued to develop his uniquely individualistic trumpet artistry until his death in 1967. His résumé reads like the proverbial *Who's Who* of jazz greats of his generation, in terms both of the leaders he worked for and the many musicians he hired for his own groups.

Nick's, the Village Vanguard, Café Society, and Other Venues

The Village Vanguard, which was opened at Charles Street and 7th Avenue by Max Gordon in 1934 and moved the next year to its present location, 178 7th Avenue, thrives in the 1990s under the management of his widow, Lorraine Gordon. The club featured poets, comedians, folk singers, and cabaret acts during its first two decades. Jazz was occasionally booked during this period and the club became exclusively a jazz venue in the mid-1950s.

Pianist Joe Sullivan, a Chicagoan who came to New York in the late 1920s, had wide experience in big bands, combos, and as a solo performer. In 1939 and 1940 he formed several integrated small bands that enjoyed residencies at New York clubs, including Café Society Downtown, The Famous Door, and the Village Vanguard. Lester Young, who had left the Basie band two weeks before, dropped in on this Sunday afternoon Vanguard jam session on December 29, 1940, and is seen here intently observing Joe's keyboard skills. The drummer is Harold "Doc" West. Trombonist J. C. Higginbotham wears the suit on the left edge of the photo. Obscured by Sullivan is trumpeter Shad Collins.

"I got a lot of kicks sitting in at . . . Minton's, the Village Vanguard, Nick's. . . . I made it out to the Coast and my brother Lee and I started a band together [and] brought it east to Café Society. . . . After that I was back with Count again out on the Coast," recalled Lester of the period December 1940, when he left Count Basie's band, to October 1944, when he was inducted into the army.[4]

A major American performing artist, songster Huddie Ledbetter, more familiarly known as Leadbelly, settled in New York in the mid-1930s and by the early 1940s was a star of the folk-singing circuit. Leadbelly had, in 1939, the year before this photo was taken, spent eight months at New York's Riker's Island prison for third-degree assault. He had earlier served prison terms in Texas and his native Louisiana on convictions for acts of violence, including murder. He is shown here during a 1940 engagement at the Village Vanguard.

Another hoary figure from the past, trumpeter Bunk Johnson had been musically inactive for a half-dozen years when in the late 1930s he was found working as a truck driver in Louisiana. On the basis of his documented associations with pioneer jazz figures, along with his later-to-be-discounted claim that he had enjoyed early-century membership in the legendary Buddy Bolden's band, Bunk was catapulted to national fame via feature articles in popular magazines. Notwithstanding his early substantial accomplishments and the major role he played in the New Orleans Revival of the 1940s, Bunk's comeback was somewhat marred by egotism and other personality problems, heavy drinking, and a failure to completely recover his former skills of execution. Still, his artistry often overcame these shortcomings both in public performance and on his 1940s recordings, which serve as an important window into many stylistic aspects of early New Orleans jazz.

Bunk was captured here during one of Charles Peterson's rare shoots outside New York City. In the first of two brief returns to jazz photography (the other would be in 1950–51), Peterson flew to Boston in 1945 and caught Johnson and Sidney Bechet at the Savoy Café, where the trumpeter was from early March into early April a member of the great reed player's quintet. The two musicians had become friends some four decades earlier in New Orleans.

Bassist Pops Foster can be partially seen in the photo's upper left corner. Not in the picture are pianist Ray Parker and drummer George Thompson. Bunk's month-long stay with the band attracted visits by some jazz-press heavies, including Nat Hentoff, Bill Russell, Gene Williams, and Ralph Gleason, as well as other prominent supporters of the art form. A trio led by saxophonist Pete Brown, a widely experienced player whose career stretched from the late teens into the early 1960s, alternated sets with the Bechet quintet.

EDDIE CONDON

By the early 1930s, having relocated from Chicago to New York, Eddie Condon had begun to establish himself as the nucleus of a large group of musicians, white and black, who played under a banner designated Chicago Jazz, Nicksieland, or simply Condon-Style. From disparate musical backgrounds and far-flung origins, these musicians played at Condon's club, were featured in concerts he had a hand in producing, took part in recording sessions organized by him, and benefited by virtue of his extraordinary promotional skills. And, their generation having been molded by Prohibition, they drank with him, often to considerable excess.

Indefatigable in his zeal to spread the word about jazz, Condon wrote a newspaper column, gave exposure to many musicians on his weekly radio show, was the first to produce jazz on television, co-authored three volumes of memoirs, and courted potential jazz patrons among the rich and famous.

He is seen here at Eddie Condon's, which he opened in 1945 at 47 West 3rd Avenue. In truth, once he became a "saloon keeper," Condon was more often at table with club guests than on the bandstand. The club, with interregna and two relocations, survived into the mid-1980s, a dozen years after its founder's death. This and the following scenes at the club were taken in 1951 during the second of Charles Peterson's two brief returns to jazz photography.

Condon and his club manager Pete Pesci bend elbows. In the background is a mosaic of Peterson's photos highlighting Condon's New York years.

The line-up, from left, is Cutty Cutshall, Wild Bill Davison, Condon, Edmond Hall, Buzzy Drootin (at drums behind Hall), bassist Bob Casey, and the eldest of intermission pianist Ralph Sutton's three sons, Jeff, who went on to become a drummer in a rock group.

Drummer Gene Krupa sits in with Eddie Condon, trombonist Lou McGarity, and Wild Bill Davison. Note the refreshments on the drum head.

Wild Bill Davison, about thirty years into his nearly seven-decade career, and clarinetist Edmond Hall, who came to New York from his native New Orleans in the late 1920s and worked in the big bands of Claude Hopkins and Lucky Millinder. Hall's versatility and distinctive sound caused him to be much sought after for combo work of both the traditional and swing genres. Davison and Hall were fixtures at Eddie Condon's club: Wild Bill from 1945 for a dozen years, Ed for the first half of the 1950s, after which he spent three years with Louis Armstrong's All Stars. The bassist in the background is probably Bob Casey.

Eddie and saloon proprietor Tim Costello at Condon's. Costello's, at 44th Street and 3rd Avenue, was a favorite hangout for jazz musicians, writers, and artists, including humorist James Thurber, some of whose cartoons decorated its walls.

Condon and Johnny Windhurst. Only eighteen when Sidney Bechet hired him in 1945 to replace Bunk Johnson at the Savoy Café in Boston, this very talented trumpeter worked at Eddie Condon's club off and on during the 1950s.

Intermission pianist at Eddie Condon's from the late 1940s through the mid–1950s, Ralph Sutton has been, along with the late Dick Wellstood, one of the few who have carried on the stride piano tradition with distinction.

Nick's, the Village Vanguard, Café Society, and Other Venues

Pianist Joe Bushkin's varied career has seen him with, to name only a few, Bunny Berigan, Joe Marsala, Tommy Dorsey, Benny Goodman, Eddie Condon, and Bing Crosby; in films and on stage, radio, and television; and raising thoroughbred horses. Here we see him in November 1950 at The Embers, on East 54th Street, where he did a long residency with his quartet. Master arranger Buck Clayton is on trumpet and Bill Goodall is on bass. Mel Tormé, already established as a singer but still marketing his early acquired drumming skills, is sitting in. Jo Jones was the regular drummer and Milt Hinton the bassist for the commencement of this engagement; Jones may have still been in the combo at this time.

Former Basie stellar soloist Buck Clayton had fond memories of The Embers. "It seemed to me that I should be paying the management for having such a good time. . . . The clientele . . . was something like seeing so many movie stars together . . .

and they were all jazz conscious." Among those he remembered as regular patrons of the club were Jackie Gleason, Art Carney, José Ferrer and Rosemary Clooney, Signe Hasso, Sylvia Syms, Peggy Lee, Robert Ruark, and Tallulah Bankhead.[5]

The Art Tatum Trio was the other half of the bill during part of the Bushkin quartet's stay at The Embers, with John Collins on guitar and Slam Stewart on bass.

The Red Norvo Trio had just begun a year-long engagement at The Embers in 1951, when this picture was taken. A year or so before, self-taught guitar virtuoso Tal Farlow had replaced Mundell Lowe in the trio and the bass player had left as well. Red set about locating Charles Mingus to replace him. He found Mingus carrying mail in Los Angeles. The great bassist, leader, composer, and major innovator had by that time already been active professionally for a decade, having played in the bands of Barney Bigard, Louis Armstrong, and Lionel Hampton.

Bill Goodall recalls the circumstances of this bizarre sidewalk scene. Charles Mingus' new bass had arrived from the West Coast and he solicited a "second opinion" as to its adequacy from Bill. Mingus, bow in hand, closely observes as the other bassist puts the instrument through its paces.[6]

From the left, Tal Farlow, Red Norvo, and the "greeter" from the El Morocco club across the street watch. On the right is Dr. Fred Sklow, a dentist who loved the music and numbered many jazz musicians among his patients. The woman is a friend of Goodall.

By the time this picture of five members of vibra-phonist Terry Gibbs' sextet was taken on July 17, 1951, at Café Society Downtown, its leader had already worked for Tommy Dorsey, Benny Good-man, and Woody Herman. He soon formed his own big band and is still going strong in the 1990s. From the left: Hal McKusick, clarinet; Sid Bulkin, drums; Jimmy Johnson, bass; Gibbs; Harry Biss, piano.

CONCERT HALL VENUES

Night clubs were not the only sites where small band and combo jazz flourished during this period. Indeed, elements of jazz had been present, albeit in diluted forms, on both European and domestic concert stages as early as the teens of the century. During that decade, ragtime and African-American dance music were being presented in concert under the batons of Will Marion Cook, James Reese Europe, and other black conductors. The pit bands of the vaudeville stage and movie houses had for some years used jazz musicians. And in 1924 Paul Whiteman brought concertized jazz into New York's Aeolian Hall with his "An Experiment in Modern Music."

However, jazz per se did not make its way into the concert hall until 1938 when the Benny Goodman band and guests from the bands of Duke Ellington and Count Basie (including the Count himself) appeared at Carnegie Hall. It was this event that opened the doors of concert halls to jazz. Later that year, John Hammond presented the first of his "Spirituals to Swing" concerts at Carnegie Hall. Also that year, Ethel Waters gave a recital there and W. C. Handy's 65th birthday was celebrated on its stage by Lionel Hampton, Teddy Wilson, Jimmie Lunceford, and others. For reasons unknown, Charles Peterson photographed neither the Goodman Carnegie Hall event nor the 1938 and 1939 "Spirituals to Swing" concerts.

THE IMPERIAL THEATRE EXTRAVAGANZA

While the 1938 Carnegie Hall evening alluded to above was a landmark event in terms of jazz invading the hitherto exclusively symphonic and operatic sancta sanctorum, the Imperial Theatre concert that was produced two years earlier, on May 24, 1936, by Joe Helbock, proprietor of the Onyx Club, can truly be considered a watershed in terms of the presentation of multiple jazz programs to large audiences. Promoted as "New York's First Swing Music Concert," the sold-out extravaganza brought together an array of jazz talent the like of which had never before gathered under one roof. This sort of copious offering would more and more become standard fare and today is commonplace, especially on the international jazz festival circuit.

Scheduled to perform at the Imperial Theatre on that evening were groups under the leadership of

Louis Armstrong, Bunny Berigan, Bob Crosby, Tommy Dorsey, Red Nichols, Red Norvo (with singer Mildred Bailey), Adrian Rollini, Artie Shaw, Stuff Smith, Joe Venuti (with guest soloist Jerry Colonna on trombone), and Wingy Manone. Also on the program were the Original Memphis Five with Phil Napoleon and Miff Mole, Frank Chase and His Saxophone Sextette, Glen Gray and the Casa Loma Orchestra, boogie woogie pianist Meade Lux Lewis, harpist Casper Reardon, a guitar duo of Carl Kress and Dick McDonough, and a contingent from the orchestra of Paul Whiteman that included trombonist Jack Teagarden and saxophonist Frankie Trumbauer. Many of the musicians who participated had been regulars at Onyx jam sessions.

"I thought it might be a good idea if I were to dream up something just a tiny bit different, just for the hell of it," Artie Shaw recalled in explanation of his decision to appear with a four-member string ensemble plus guitar and drums.[7] Shaw, who had turned twenty-six the day before the concert and up to now had worked only as a sideman and studio musician, was astonished at the ovation accorded the group's single rehearsed number, "Interlude in B Flat," which they were compelled to repeat as the evening's lone encore. The clarinetist put together his first big band later that year and was soon a star of the Swing Era.

The part of the line-up we see here with Shaw is probably first violinist Harry Bluestone (left) and cellist Rudy Simms. Not shown are Mannie Green, violin; Izzie Zir, viola; Carl Kress, guitar; and Arthur Stein, drums. This photo later hung on the wall of the Onyx.

Stuff Smith and his Onyx Club Band were the accompanists at the Imperial Theatre concert for Beverly "Baby" White, who would make her first recordings the next year with the Claude Hopkins Orchestra.

Much-in-demand guitarists Dick McDonough and Carl Kress performed at the Imperial concert in duo, a format they had established several years earlier.

"I was unprepared for such a tremendous thrill," wrote critic Helen Oakley of Bunny Berigan in her review of a June 1935 performance of the Benny Goodman band in Milwaukee. "The man is a master. I doubt if I ever heard a more forceful trumpet, with unending ideas and possessed of that quality peculiar to both Teagarden and Armstrong, that of swinging the band as a whole at the outset and carrying it solidly along with him, without a letup, until the finish of his chorus. Bunny is, I believe, the only trumpeter comparable to Louis Armstrong."[8] For trumpeter Pee Wee Erwin, Berigan "was one of the greatest trumpet players who ever lived. I don't think to this day I've ever heard a sheer sound on the instrument which is as impressive as Bunny Berigan's. . . . It was just an overwhelming sound . . . , to say nothing of the wonderful ideas that he played."[9] Berigan, an alcoholic since his early twenties, died of cirrhosis of the liver in 1942 at the age of 33.

For his Imperial Theatre appearance Berigan fronted the Red McKenzie–Eddie Condon group he was then in residence with at 52nd Street's Club 18. At far left is Artie Shaw, who filled in for ailing tenor saxophonist Forrest Crawford. Condon is on guitar, Morty Stuhlmaker at the bass. Not in the photo are pianist Joe Bushkin and drummer Sam Weiss. According to the printed program, comb player McKenzie did not participate in the concert.

Fats Waller was booked into Carnegie Hall for January 14, 1942. It was another milestone in the history of jazz, for this was the first time an individual jazz artist had been the featured performer at the august venue. According to the program, Fats would play his own compositions at the piano, choosing spontaneously from almost a hundred listed titles, and then perform a selection of spirituals at the Hammond organ. Trumpeter Hot Lips Page was scheduled for a blues piece with him and a small band would join the pianist at the end for a finale medley. For several hours before curtain time a dozen or so well-wishing friends hung out in Fats' dressing room—the Toscanini Suite—and partied with him. Consequently, the great pianist, severely inebriated and quaking with nervousness over his Carnegie Hall debut, took to the stage confused as to the program that he had earlier committed to memory. He offered instead two rambling and sometimes repetitive sets. Although Fats' incapacitated state escaped the notice of many in his admiring audience, the evening nevertheless barely avoided collapsing into a shambles.

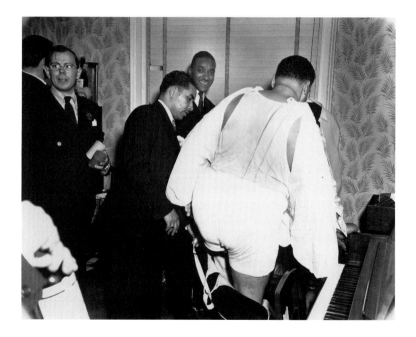

Fats is being helped into his tuxedo before the concert. At left in glasses is adman-turned-jazz-promoter Ernie Anderson, who conceived the idea for the concert and organized it.

The pianist, somewhat unsteady on his feet after a few more tastes during intermission, flashes a smile for the camera as he is escorted back to the stage by an apprehensive Anderson.

Fats Waller seated at the Carnegie Hall Steinway.

The concert's musical director Eddie Condon, on the far left, and his hand-picked all-star assemblage. Tenorist Bud Freeman came down from Chicago for the concert, bassist John Kirby absented himself for a spell from the club where he was leading his sextet, drummer Gene Krupa made arrangements to finish a little early at the Paramount Theatre where his big band was breaking attendance records, and clarinetist Pee Wee Russell (and Condon) skipped a set at Nick's. Trumpeter Max Kaminsky was currently with Artie Shaw's band (as was Hot Lips Page), which was apparently unengaged on this date.

In what turned out to be, for critics and audience alike, the evening's highlight, Hot Lips Page sang a blues and then topped it off with some plunger-muted horn that brought the house down.

With the declaration of war a scant few weeks earlier, it had become routine to close concerts with the "Star Spangled Banner." The problem was that as the number got underway it seemed for a moment that none of the musicians could recall the middle part of the national anthem. Maxie looks relieved as the ever-resourceful Pee Wee, supported by Gene's appropriately stirring snare drum action, remembers the melody line and saves the day.

Shortly after the Fats Waller concert Ernie Anderson and Eddie Condon conceived the idea of presenting informal jazz sessions in Town Hall. They booked the venue at 5:30 P.M. for two hours on a Saturday night in February and assembled more than a dozen musicians for the event. Three more concerts followed through April of that year and the series resumed in the fall, continuing into the spring of 1947. Most of the musicians involved had played with each other at clubs or in jam sessions.

Pictured here at a Town Hall concert in 1942 are pianist Dave Bowman, Condon, clarinetist Rod Cless, bassist Al Morgan, Pee Wee Russell, drummer Zutty Singleton, and Max Kaminsky. That the musicians were cooking as Charles Peterson clicked his camera's shutter is the message of the action he captured. Note in particular guitarist Condon's "pedal extremity," to borrow from the verbal coinage of Fats Waller. James P. Johnson provided intermission piano. Others who participated in these Town Hall concerts over the years included Sidney Bechet, Joe Sullivan, Ed Hall, Big Sid Catlett, Hot Lips Page, trumpeter Muggsy Spanier, clarinetist Irving Fazola, Henry "Red" Allen, pianist Mel Powell, and drummer Kansas Fields.

In a development that both looked to the past, when jazz bands entertained on riverboats plying the Mississippi and its tributaries, and foreshadowed the jazz cruise scene of the 1980s and 1990s, jazz historian, lecturer, radio show host, and record and concert producer Rudi Blesh and Russian-born Chicagoan, combo leader, and master of piano blues Art Hodes co-produced in the summer of 1946 "Jazz on the River," four-hour weekend evening cruises up and down the Hudson for a $3 fare. In addition to the musicians Peterson shot on the one evening he spent aboard the craft, Wild Bill Davison, Ralph Sutton, Sidney Bechet, and Hodes were some of the others who worked these floating gigs that resumed for part of the summer of 1947.

Guitarist Danny Barker and bassist Pops Foster accompany the pianist as two horns lie idle on the upright.

Clarinetist Albert Nicholas takes a solo. Nicholas, Barker, and Foster, all from New Orleans, relocated in New York after substantial early professional activity in their native city and went on to big band and combo work under many prominent leaders. Sixteen-year-old trumpeter Johnny Glasel is above Nicholas' left shoulder. Glasel, who would record later that year with Bob Wilber's Wildcats, went on to work with Benny Goodman, Woody Herman, and others and was president of New York Local 802 of the American Federation of Musicians from 1983 through 1992.

Nick's, the Village Vanguard, Café Society, and Other Venues

James P. Johnson strides at the keyboard behind a front-line of trumpeter Marty Marsala and Albert Nicholas. Baby Dodds is on drums, Danny Barker on guitar.

New Orleans–born Baby Dodds' musical history begins in the teens and reaches into the 1950s and involved him with Bunk Johnson, King Oliver, Jelly Roll Morton, Louis Armstrong, Sidney Bechet, and many other legends, a label that of course equally applies to him.

Dan Burley had played the Chicago rent party scene in the 1920s and then turned to journalism, becoming an editor with the *New York Amsterdam News*. If Burley was not the pianist on the gig, perhaps he was covering "Jazz on the River" for the paper and then sat in. He also recorded for Rudi Blesh's Circle label at about this time.

A victim of the dissipation to which so many of the jazz musicians of his era succumbed, Pee Wee Russell collapsed on New Year's Eve, 1950, on the bandstand of Coffee Dan's in San Francisco. Chronic alcoholism and severe malnutrition had rendered him critically ill with acute pancreatitis and, as an indigent, he was placed in the charity ward of San Francisco County Hospital. At the age of forty-four and weighing in at seventy-three pounds, Pee Wee appeared to be very near death. However, after a number of blood transfusions, surgery, and two months' hospitalization the clarinetist was released and put aboard a flight to New York.

Meanwhile, Life magazine ran a story on Pee Wee's sad circumstances with a photo of Louis Armstrong and Jack Teagarden visiting him in the hospital. Benefits were held to raise money for his medical expenses, one at San Francisco's Hangover Club with Armstrong's All Stars heading the bill and a second one at Town Hall in New York under the auspices of Eddie Condon. A third benefit took place in Chicago in March. The recovering clarinetist was presented a total of $4500 from the three fund-raisers.

Welcoming home a ravaged Pee Wee at New York's La Guardia Airport on February 27, 1951, after closing Eddie Condon's at 4 A.M. and staying up the rest of the morning are pianist Gene Schroeder (standing, far left), bassist Bob Casey, drummer Buzzy Drootin (standing, background), Condon, and Ralph Sutton. Photographer Charles Peterson (kneeling, foreground) arranged his subjects and then had long-time Condon friend and sometime suitcase drummer Josh Billings click the shutter.

Taking better care of his health, Pee Wee lived another eighteen years. His death in 1969 at the age of sixty-two was caused by chronic pancreatitis and cirrhosis of the liver.

Nick's, the Village Vanguard, Café Society, and Other Venues   109

Willie the Lion Smith was one of the more than thirty musicians who affirmed their personal friendship and professional respect for the great clarinet player by performing at the Pee Wee Russell benefit concert at Town Hall on February 21, 1951. In addition to those pictured at the airport, there were trumpeters Red Allen, Billy Butterfield, and Pee Wee Erwin; cornetist Wild Bill Davison; trombonists Cutty Cutshall, Lou McGarity, Vernon Brown, Frank Orchard, and Jimmy Archey; clarinetists Ed Hall and Peanuts Hucko; baritone saxophonist Ernie Caceres; pianists Joe Sullivan and Joe Bushkin; bassist Al Hall; drummers George Wettling and Ray McKinley; and singer Lee Wiley.

The benefit at Town Hall. Note the all-white audience. With rare exceptions the downtown venues excluded blacks. Not so the stage and bandstand, whereon mixed groups affirmed that jazz musicians were years in advance of the times. Third row, third and fourth from right are magazine picture editor Helen "Daisy" Decker and pulp writer Duane Decker (with glasses), close friends of Pee Wee.

At a jam session in August 1939 organized for a Life magazine feature: Eddie Condon, guitar; J. C. Higginbotham, trombone; record producer Harry Lim (seated); Rex Stewart, cornet; Brad Gowans, valve trombone; Max Kaminsky and Hot Lips Page, trumpet; Pee Wee Russell, clarinet; and Ernie Anderson (behind Pee Wee). One wonders whether Pee Wee was getting any help from another reed or two off camera.

CHAPTER 4

Jam Sessions

Neither formal instruction nor book learning makes a jazz musician. Rather, from its very beginnings, the idiom has been learned by ear, by close observation of mentors, and by competition with one's peers. The informal get-together has always played a major role in the process: early-century band battles on the streets of New Orleans[1]; the "head cuttin' " contests of Delta bluesmen[2]; Prohibition Era Chicago sit-ins in the backroom of the Liberty Inn, and interracial jam sessions at Sam Beer's My Cellar[3]; those legendary all-night blowing sessions in wide-open Kansas City of the 1930s[4]; the nightly face-off of stride pianists in pre-war Harlem's after-hours joints[5]; the bebop crucible of Minton's Playhouse in the 1940s[6]; the sessions at L.A.'s Club Alabam and other Central Avenue clubs in the 1950s[7]; the regular meetings of the Association for the Advancement of Creative Musicians (AACM) in Chicago in the 1960s[8]; the New York loft scene of the 1970s[9]; and in the 1980s a resuscitated jam session scene at the Blue Note and other Manhattan clubs, lauded by young trumpeter Philip Harper as having been "probably one of my better learning experiences. . . . Sometimes in one night you could make your rounds and hit about four or five sessions."[10] These are some of the contexts in which musicians have come together in an—if not always impromptu—at least informal fashion. In this chapter we look in on some typical New York jam session scenes of the late 1930s and early 1940s.

Commodore record label producer Milt Gabler, who had earlier helped organize several jam sessions that took place in recording studios, soon conceived the idea of holding them in clubs on 52nd Street. Accordingly, he held one featuring Bessie Smith at The Famous Door and then began sponsoring Sunday afternoon sessions at Jimmy Ryan's. Admission—initially 65¢, later $1.00—was charged, drinks were sold, and the musicians were paid union scale. The high regard in which these gatherings were held, by both participants and audience, is nicely summed up by trumpeter

Max Kaminsky. "There was a moment there, in 1941–1942, at the Ryan sessions, when hot jazz seemed at its purest. . . . When a musician was building a solo you never heard a sound from the audience. . . . The feeling was that musicians and fans alike lived for Sundays."[11] By 1950 or so, the regularly scheduled New York club jam session depicted in the following pages had run its course and virtually went out of existence, not to bloom again in New York for more than three decades.

The line-up at this Jimmy Ryan's session on November 23, 1941, was Eddie Condon, guitar;

George Wettling, drums; Sandy Williams, trombone; Bobby Hackett, cornet; Max Kaminsky, trumpet; Pee Wee Russell, clarinet; Joe Sullivan, piano; and Al Morgan, bass.

Gabler saw to it that the sessions were integrated, pairing a Condon-led group (itself often mixed) with a band made up of Harlem musicians. Once the session got underway, of course, musicians found themselves crossing back and forth, as so many of these scenes attest. This session was at

Jimmy Ryan's on February 1, 1942. Gabler is at far left with finger to mouth and to the left of him is his cousin Leonard Krauser. The trumpeters are Henry "Red" Allen (second from the left), Max Kaminsky (standing in the rear at far left), Marty Marsala (right foreground), and Hot Lips Page (standing, rear center). The saxophonists are Kenny Hollon (wearing glasses), tenor, and Pete Brown, alto. Zutty Singleton is on drums; Jack Bland, guitar; Earl Hines, piano; and Al Morgan, bass. The trumpeter to the left of "Red" Allen is unknown.

George Wettling, a mainstay at Eddie Condon's club and a frequent participant in the jam sessions at Ryan's, November 9, 1941.

At Ryan's on January 19, 1941, are J. C. Higginbotham, trombone; Brad Gowans, valve trombone; Jack Bland, guitar; Pee Wee Russell, clarinet; Henry "Red" Allen and Hot Lips Page, trumpet; Bill King, bass; and Edmond Hall, clarinet.

From the left: Ike Quebec, tenor saxophone; Jack Bland, guitar (behind Bailey); Buster Bailey and Pee Wee Russell, clarinet; Billy Kyle, piano; Charlie Shavers, trumpet; Vic Dickenson trombone; and Al Morgan, bass. Note the nice shadow effect to the left of Shavers. Jimmy Ryan's, November 9, 1941.

J. C. Higginbotham, trombone; Hot Lips Page, trumpet; and Jack Bland, guitar. The drummer sitting in is twenty-year-old Jackie Cooper, prominent in his younger years in "Our Gang" films and in later life in several television series. Jimmy Ryan's, February 1, 1942.

Under the watchful eyes of Milt Gabler and Zutty Singleton, Dr. Fred Sklow, the jazz-loving dentist who maintained many a horn player's embouchure, pours a drink, perhaps for himself, perhaps for the drummer. Jimmy Ryan's, February 1, 1942.

Lips Page stands to the left of trombonist Sandy Williams, Albert Nicholas and Pee Wee Russell are the clarinetists, Zutty Singleton is on drums, and Brad Gowans on valve trombone. Jimmy Ryan's, February 1, 1942.

Charles Peterson's explanation for the amusement of Eddie Condon and Bobby Hackett, flanking Pee Wee, was that the clarinetist got so involved in his solo he couldn't conclude it in time to join the resumed ensemble. Some remarks of Wild Bill Davison are relevant: "I think there was no clarinet player that ever lived who knew how to play a last chorus or an ensemble like he did. He could always find the right note. . . . I always thought sometimes he would never finish what he got started, but he always did somehow."[12]

This scene—to which some fanciful interpretations have been given, e.g., that Max Kaminsky was home on a 72-hour pass from the *army*—is actually a send-up. The date is February 16, 1941, and Max would not enter the service—as a trumpeter with Artie Shaw's U.S. Navy band—for another seven months. In the vestibule of Ryan's, surrounded by old friends, drink and cigarette in hand, Max is modeling pre-war enlister and bassist Bill King's overseas cap and overcoat. Note the ill fit of the coat, the bunched-up sleeve, and Maxie's white shirt. Peterson's sense of humor is on display here in more ways than one, for the nicely framed woman on the "Automatic Hostess" appears to be enjoying the spoof along with the others, leaving Maxie the lone sober-faced member in this wry group portrait. On the left are Eddie Condon and Sidney Bechet; Hot Lips Page is on the far right.

In addition to those musicians pictured in the foregoing scenes at Jimmy Ryan's, others participated in the jam sessions there, including Lester Young; Billie Holiday; Wild Bill Davison; Pops Foster; trumpeter Sidney de Paris; reed players Sidney Bechet, Coleman Hawkins, Ben Webster, Chu Berry, Mezz Mezzrow, Eddie Barefield, Rod Cless, and Happy Caldwell; trombonists Wilbur de Paris and Miff Mole; pianists James P. Johnson, Joe Sullivan, Art Hodes, Cliff Jackson, and Sammy Price; and drummers Jo Jones and Kansas Fields.

Many clubs featured weekly jam sessions, including the Onyx Club, Café Society Downtown, the Hickory House, and The Famous Door. At another, the Village Vanguard, resident pianist Joe Sullivan hosts a session on December 29, 1940.

J. C. Higginbotham is on trombone; Harold "Doc" West, drums; Shad Collins, trumpet; and Lester Young, tenor saxophone. Collins and West were members of a working combo Young put together at this time.

An out-of-town site where jam sessions regularly took place was the Greenhaven Inn on Route 1 in Mamaroneck, New York. Drummer Zutty Singleton was often a participant, as was Hot Lips Page (behind cowbell). To the left of Lips is valve trombonist Brad Gowans.

In an effort to bring the music to a wider circle of society, Eddie Condon and two friends of his who worked in advertising, Ernie Anderson and Paul Smith, sought a Madison Avenue–area venue for jam sessions. Pictured here is the ballroom of the Park Lane, a staid residential hotel on Park Avenue where, during 1938 and early 1939, The Friday Club sessions took place.

The clarinetist holding forth here on February 17, 1939, is Joe Marsala. Seated, from the left, are Bud Freeman, Hot Lips Page, trumpeter Sterling Bose, Eddie Condon, and Pee Wee Russell. Bobby Hackett stands at the far right. Not shown are pianist Arthur Schutt, bassist Morty Stuhlmaker, and drummer Zutty Singleton.

"For the first session I got twenty-two musicians," Condon recalled. "It was an upsetting experience for the Park Lane. The cocktail lounge . . . ran out of Scotch, waiters, ice, and several other natural resources. Every seat was occupied, and the applause was in the ovation bracket. The next week we had another sell-out; we settled down to what we hoped would be a long and successful run. During the fifth session, two vice-presidents of the New York Central Railroad [who owned the hotel] walked into the cocktail lounge and ordered drinks." Horrified at the "noise" emanating from the ballroom, they forbade future sessions on the premises and fired the manager who had approved the leasing of the room.[13]

Eddie Condon, Pee Wee Russell, Bobby Hackett, Sterling Bose, Morty Stuhlmaker, Hot Lips Page, Bud Freeman, and Joe Marsala. Arthur Schutt is above Freeman's left hand. Zutty Singleton's drums are behind Hackett and Bose. Seated at the far left behind Pee Wee is Marty Marsala. February 17, 1939.

Sultry-voiced Lee Wiley, who was briefly married to pianist Jess Stacy, worked with both big bands and combos. Here she is backed by the same group as above, minus the trumpets. Joe Marsala, who emceed at some of The Friday Club sessions, is at the far right. February 24, 1939.

Pianist Willie the Lion Smith, here with Zutty Singleton (far right), Bud Freeman (far left), and Bobby Hackett, was at the February 17, 1939, session.

Billie Holiday at The Friday Club, February 24, 1939, the same session at which Lee Wiley sang. Joe Marsala sits on the left and Bud Freeman on the right of Billie. Arthur Schutt can be seen in far right center.

Sidney Bechet, Fats Waller, Henry "Red" Allen, Jimmy Dorsey, Big Sid Catlett, Max Kaminsky, Leo Watson, and Teddy Bunn were some of the others who performed at the short-lived Friday Club sessions.

An historic jam session organized by jazz critic Helen Oakley, at the Brunswick studio, Sunday, March 14, 1937. The musicians are, from the left, Marty Marsala, George Wettling, Eddie Condon, Joe Marsala, and Joe Bushkin. Among the many others participating were Duke Ellington, Count Basie, Lester Young, Chick Webb, Ella Fitzgerald, Rex Stewart, Benny Goodman, Gene Krupa, Artie Shaw, Buck Clayton, Walter Page, Freddie Green, Hot Lips Page, Herschel Evans, Billy Kyle, Mezz Mezzrow, Graham Forbes, and Frankie Newton.

In addition to the sporadic jam sessions in recording studios and the regularly scheduled ones at clubs, there were ad hoc invitation-only sessions. A prominent example was an August 1939 gathering put together by Eddie Condon and Ernie Anderson at the request of *Life* magazine and held at the Riverside Drive penthouse studio apartment of Hearst newspapers political cartoonist Burris Jenkins. Alexander King and other editors at *Life* had been delighted with Charles Peterson's photos for a special feature on jazz the year before (see Chapter 5) and they wanted to do a follow-up. The photo spread was intended for the magazine's popular "*Life* Goes to a Party" series and Peterson was called in to shoot it. (Unfortunately, the article never ran.)

Duke Ellington is at the piano in the foreground with Eddie Condon, on guitar, to the right. Behind are trombonists J. C. Higginbotham, Brad Gowans, and Juan Tizol; trumpeter Cootie Williams; cornetist Rex Stewart; and trumpeter Max Kaminsky. Standing behind Max is Harry Lim, who had come to the United States a few months before from his native Java, Indonesia. Soon after he arrived here, Lim began producing jam sessions in New York and Chicago, and in 1943 he began a four-decade career as a record producer, at first for Keynote and then for other labels. According to Charles Peterson, both as recorded in his notes and as told to his son Don, twenty-year-old Lim was the guest of honor at the bash.

From the left: Hot Lips Page and Max Kaminsky have trumpets to mouth; bassist Clyde Newcombe has his back to the door jamb; J. C. Higginbotham is on trombone; Harry Lim is leaning on the piano; and Cozy Cole is behind Lim on drums. In the background, host Burris Jenkins holds his hands up and Eddie Condon is looking to the left toward tenorist Chu Berry. Rex Stewart has trumpet to mouth in center, Duke Ellington is playing Rosetta Tharpe's guitar, a French guest drinks from a bottle, and Johnny Hodges plays alto on the far right. In the foreground, with backs to camera, are, from the left: Ellington band vocalist Ivie Anderson; Cab Calloway; and Sister Rosetta Tharpe (playing piano). The man sitting in the right background is journalist Hubbell Young of the *New York Times*.

Duke and Sister Rosetta, clearly enjoying themselves and each other, are back on their proper instruments now as Lips and Cab look on. Juan Tizol, trombone in hand (note its shadow, reflected by the photographer's flash), peeks over Lips' shoulder. Condon is to the right of Cab.

Jam Sessions

Cozy Cole stirs up the action for, from left, J. C. Higginbotham, Clyde Newcombe, Rex Stewart, Max Kaminsky, and Hot Lips Page as Billie Holiday, Harry Lim, and Eddie Condon observe.

The informality of the occasion is splendidly captured in this shot of Bud Freeman and Duke Ellington. Those looking on are unknown.

Bud Freeman, Johnny Hodges, and Chu Berry get it together. When tenor saxophonist Berry was fatally injured in an automobile accident in 1941 at the age of thirty-one, he was already approaching the artistry of Coleman Hawkins and Lester Young. Hodges was the greatest alto saxophonist of his era. Freeman was the first jazz tenor saxophonist, black or white, to fashion a style wholly independent from Coleman Hawkins' reigning influence.

Lips Page, Harry Lim, pianist Dave Bowman,
bassist Clyde Newcombe, Billie Holiday, and the
French guest.

As Eddie Condon, Clyde Newcombe, Billie Holiday, and Ernie Anderson (in dark glasses) look on, the French guest tries out Max Kaminsky's horn, accompanied by Dave Bowman, piano, and Max, drums. In the background, from left, are Bud Freeman, J. C. Higginbotham, and Harry Lim.

Dave Tough was a member of the Austin High School Gang, the young whites who were inspired by the New Orleans Rhythm Kings, King Oliver, Louis Armstrong, Johnny Dodds, Baby Dodds, Jimmie Noone, and others, and in the 1920s put together their own Chicago Style. A leading drummer of his time, Tough was versatile enough to excel in settings as varied as Condon-style groups; the orchestras of Bunny Berigan, Tommy Dorsey, and Benny Goodman; and the progressive band of Woody Herman.

Eddie Condon and Cozy Cole are to the right. The man on the far right is unknown.

J. C. Higginbotham, Rex Stewart, Brad Gowans, and Hot Lips Page get it on.

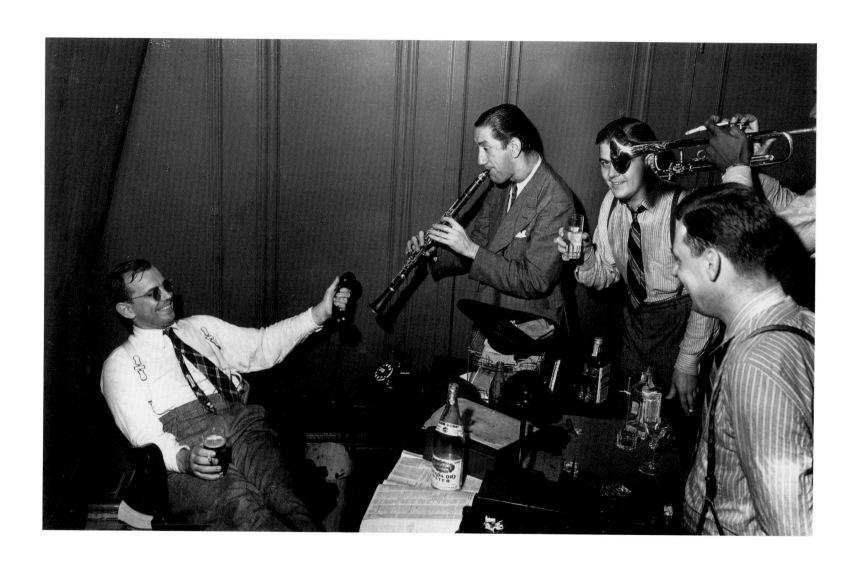

A never-ending game for the musicians who worked at Nick's was being fired at the end of the evening and then hired back on the morrow. Here Ernie Anderson has Nick Rongetti on the telephone as Pee Wee Russell affords inimitable proof that he is indeed at the *Life* jam session and not off carousing. Recognizing the eight bars of clarinet as none other than Pee Wee's, Nick withdraws his threat to fire him "for good" and excuses him from playing the opening set that night. The obtruding trumpet is probably Lips'. Brad Gowans is at far right and the man holding the drink is pianist Dave Bowman.

Dave Tough with Cozy Cole. Camera, subjects, and perhaps the photographer are out of focus here. Dave Tough, intellectually preoccupied and a frustrated writer, was among those jazz artists of his era who suffered most severely from the idiom's vocational affliction of alcoholism. His death in 1948 was caused by a fractured skull resulting from a fall on the street while inebriated. He was forty-one years old.

The Walt Whitman School on East 78th Street had long exposed its young students to ballet, modern dance, foreign cinema, and other performing and visual arts. Don Peterson was enrolled in the fifth grade there and, when the school's administration decided it was time the youngsters experience in the flesh the native American art form of jazz, the photographer made arrangements for Louis Armstrong and some of the Condon crowd to hold an afternoon jam session for the elementary grades. The year was 1942.

Louis Armstrong and Bobby Hackett on, respectively, trumpet and cornet; Brad Gowans, valve trombone; and Eddie Condon, guitar. Not shown are trumpeter Max Kaminsky, clarinetist Pee Wee Russell, pianist Joe Sullivan, and drummer Zutty Singleton.

These fifth and sixth grade innocents appear to be spellbound by the charismatic Satchmo.

We know that there were frequent occasions when musicians got together off the job or during an intermission and spontaneously started blowing. But how often would a photographer have been on hand? Here we have a jam session that was put together backstage at the Paramount Theatre, where in May of 1937 Louis Armstrong's big band shared the bill with a movie. Jazz musicians, aware that having their photos in the local press and national magazines would attract patrons to their club appearances, increase record sales, and generally enhance their careers, fully cooperated when asked to participate in an "impromptu" jam session such as this one organized by Charles Peterson.

From the left: Tommy Dorsey, trombone; Bud Freeman, tenor saxophone; Pops Foster, bass; Louis Armstrong, trumpet; Eddie Condon, guitar; George Wettling, drums; and Henry "Red" Allen, trumpet.

Tommy Dorsey and Bud Freeman look on in admiration as Louis demonstrates his incomparable virtuosity cum soul. This photo ran in *Life* on August 8, 1938.

Duane Decker, a writer of sports action pulp novels and an amateur clarinetist, and Helen "Daisy" O'Brian, picture editor at *Cosmopolitan* magazine, were avid jazz fans and numbered as friends many musicians. Reciprocating their support and Helen's promotional efforts through her journalistic connections, some of their jazz-playing friends made a sixty-mile journey for a jam session at the Deckers' July 1949 wedding at the home of Charles Peterson in Easton, Pennsylvania. (The photographer had moved there after discharge from the U.S. Coast Guard in 1943.)

From the left: Frank Orchard, trombone; Pee Wee Russell, clarinet; Herb Ward, bass; Jonah Jones, trumpet; Helen Decker; Willie the Lion Smith, piano; and Duane Decker. Others making the trip were Bobby Hackett, Eddie Condon, George Wettling, and Jimmy Archey.

The bride sits in on whisk brooms and suitcase, the bridegroom on clarinet, and Charles Peterson on guitar. Herb Ward is on bass and the Lion is at the piano. Bobbie Koch, a family friend, peeks over the piano. For this photo Peterson's seventeen-year-old son Don handled his father's press camera.

Peterson, who had played banjo and guitar with several bands in the 1920s and early 1930s, resumed playing guitar in the 1960s, working weekend country club dance gigs with local bands in Sarasota, Florida, and continued to play until his death in 1976.

Taking advantage of an unusual photo opportunity, Charles Peterson took several of the musicians to nearby Nazareth, where at the Moravian Historical Society's Whitefield House resided one of the oldest organs built in the United States. Ralph Sutton, at the Tannenberg Organ, accompanies Jonah Jones as jazz historian Rudi Blesh and Willie the Lion Smith observe.

The Deckers on their own hosted many private jam sessions at their Gramercy Park apartment in the late 1940s and early 1950s. Here, on November 8, 1950, several guests marvel at the astonishing action of Earl Hines' hands. Seated to the left of Earl is pianist/entertainer Kirby Walker. The woman on the right with drink to mouth is Virginia Peterson, wife of the photographer. Seated on the far right is Allan Morrison, an editor in the New York office of *Ebony* magazine.

Technician Bridges mans the cutting lathe at Brunswick Studio for the Commodore record-ing session on April 30, 1938.

CHAPTER 5
The Recording Scene

For those whose acquaintance with recorded sound reaches no farther back than the 1950s, exposure to what was considered state-of-the-art electronic gear in the 1940s and earlier may constitute something of a shock to the system. The tape recorder was not yet in use, turntable speed was at 78 rpm, a ten-inch "side" was of three minutes' duration and a twelve-inch "side" of five, and if you dropped a record on anything harder than a pillow, your only recourse was to the dust bin.

The big record companies—RCA Victor, Columbia, Decca, Brunswick—operated their own recording studios. The independents had to make do with time and space leased from the biggies. Then, as now, it was these tiny "indies" (usually owned by individuals whose dedication to the art form of jazz amounted to nothing less than an obsession) that more often documented the cutting edge efforts of the art form. Needless to say,

the lesser known but often highly creative player stood little chance of seeing his or her name on a major label recording, or of even participating in a small group session on any but labels little known except in the jazz world, where they were the *lingua franca*.

So, while a lot of jazz was indeed captured in the recording studios of the industry giants of the day and much of it has been reissued, it is often the two-fers and boxed sets of remastered sides from such companies as Commodore, Blue Note, Keynote, Solo Art, and Hot Record Society that provide surprises of a most delightful nature.

Charles Peterson's love of jazz led him to explore not just the clubs, concert halls, and ballrooms where the music was performed, but the recording sessions where it was captured directly on disc. In the photos that follow, the photographer opens doors onto some fascinating scenes.

Milt Gabler's pioneering efforts as a record producer included several firsts. His mid-1930s United Hot Clubs of America (UHCA) releases of cutouts he purchased from Brunswick, Decca, and other companies introduced the concept of reissues to jazz; he was the founder in 1938 of the first American label devoted exclusively to jazz, Commodore (only the French Swing label, begun in 1937, preceded it); and he led the way in the listing of band personnel on record labels.

The Commodore Music Shop originally was a hardware store that Milt's father had opened before World War I. It later evolved into a radio and electrical supply store and by 1926 was carrying records. The scenes that follow are from a shoot Charles Peterson did in August 1950 for a spread on the store in *Cosmopolitan* magazine. The article, "Platter Paradise," was subtitled, "It's the hottest spot on earth for jazz fiends—and a fascinating place for anyone." Emerging from the store is singer Mindy Carson, who appeared on radio and in concert with the Paul Whiteman orchestra and later had her own radio show.

Milt Gabler's store was for many years a meeting place for jazz musicians, collectors, and fans. Here, as a customer (or perhaps a model provided by the magazine) looks on, pianist Willie the Lion Smith points out fellow music-maker Arturo Toscanini.

Singer Rosemary Clooney, who the next year would have her first hit record "Come on-a My House," holds up a Billie Holiday album.

Milt Gabler beams with pride next to a window display of releases, many of which he produced or reissued on Commodore, Decca, and other labels. In addition to operating his own label, organizing jam sessions, and running the store, Milt commenced in 1941 a three-decade career with Decca as an "A & R man" (Artist and Repertoire).

Eddie Condon with "Porkchop." Jess Stacy (at piano) and Bud Freeman are to the right. Brunswick Studio, April 30, 1938.

The first Commodore session took place on January 18, 1938, the morning after the historic Benny Goodman concert in Carnegie Hall. The session pictured here was the label's next full-band session. Eddie Condon had approached Alexander King, an editor at *Life* and regular customer at the Commodore Music Shop, and urged him to cover the session for the magazine.

"I have the photographer," the irrepressible Condon enthused. "There is a guitarist named Charlie Peterson who played with Rudy Vallee and who saved his money. He is now a professional photographer and he knows how to handle musicians. He won't bother them when he shouldn't bother them and he'll get what you want."[1] Fourteen of Peterson's photos were used in an eleven-page spread entitled "Swing: The Hottest and Best Kind of Jazz Reaches Its Golden Age," which appeared in the August 8, 1938, issue. The following three photographs are from the same session.

The great trombonist and singer Jack Teagarden, whose fluency in the blues derived from his Texas roots.

Bobby Hackett on cornet with Pee Wee Russell and Bud Freeman. Guest and amateur drummer Harry Ely seems to be momentarily filling in for George Wettling during a run-through of one of the tunes.

This photo of Pee Wee was to appear on the cover of *Life* but the feature, slated as a "photo essay," was postponed for three months and Pee Wee's arresting countenance was bumped to a full page inside. The intervening issues of *Life* were taken up with features on such subjects as labor strife, the burgeoning European and Asian conflicts, and Howard Hughes' four-day flight around the world. Covers were of Errol Flynn, Shirley Temple, a West Point wedding, a Chinese soldier standing at his post, women garment workers, and glamour shots of fashion models. The cover of the August 8 issue that ran the feature on "Swing" was of swimsuit-clad divers captured in midair over a quarry.

Perhaps Pee Wee is here playing "Serenade to a Shylock," a tune composed on the spot apropos the loan sharks awaiting the clarinetist outside. Pee Wee's clarinet had been put in hock by his live-in companion Lola, the story goes, and its retrieval for use on this occasion had been permitted only on condition that the $8 loan be settled upon the session's conclusion, when Milt Gabler paid the musicians in cash.

Billie Holiday at the April 20, 1939, Commodore session that included her riveting rendition of "Strange Fruit," a searing indictment of lynching penned by poet Lewis Allen. Columbia Records, to whom Billie was under contract, rejected her request to record the song but permitted a temporary loan of the singer to Milt Gabler for this and three other tunes. It seems fitting that trumpeter Frankie Newton, an activist in the cause of racial justice and other "radical" causes of the time, was the session's leader and arranger.

From the left: Billie, tenorist Kenneth Hollon, altoist Tab Smith, tenorist Stan Payne, and pianist Sonny White. Panama-born White, who had come up in Jesse Stone's and Willie Bryant's 1930s bands, was Billie's regular accompanist at the time of this session. Tab's career included Mississippi riverboat work in Fate Marable's band and several periods with Basie. Hollon and Payne traveled in both combo and big band circles.

Charles Peterson noted that he shot this photo as Billie was actually recording "Strange Fruit." Jimmy McLin is on guitar, Johnny Williams on bass.

The Recording Scene

This and the following three photos were shot at the March 23, 1940, "Jam Session at Commodore" in the Decca studio on West 57th Street. One tune, "A Good Man Is Hard to Find," was spread over four twelve-inch 78 rpm sides in an attempt to capture on record, if not the actual occasion, at least something akin to the essence of a jam session—the first time this had been tried. Some of the eleven musicians came straight from all-night drinking and others arrived well supplied with reinforcements. Notwithstanding the resulting confusion and nearly fifty "breakdowns" (the trade term for aborted recordings), the seventeen minutes of music captured that morning more than a half-century ago rank with the finest sides Milt Gabler and Eddie Condon did together. From the left: trombonist Miff Mole, valve trombonist Brad Gowans, cornetist Muggsy Spanier, and trumpeter Max Kaminsky.

A quintessential Chicago Style player, Spanier had in his early teens been captivated by in-person exposure to King Oliver's playing and became a professional musician several years later. Mole, a trombonist of impressive technical abilities, was among the several who began, in the early 1920s, to extend the language of the instrument beyond the New Orleans tailgate approach, developing in the process a greater agility on the horn, which in turn served as a stepping stone to the flexibility characteristic of the playing of Jimmy Harrison, Jack Teagarden, Dicky Wells, Tommy Dorsey, and others.

Tenorist Bud Freeman (middle), clarinetist Pee Wee Russell, and Joe Marsala, who is not playing clarinet, his principal instrument, but alto saxophone. The alto was rarely used in this style of jazz but was a useful tool for a reed player making part of his living working in big bands.

Pianist Jess Stacy's career included several periods with Benny Goodman, membership in many other big bands, and work as a single. His solo on "Sing Sing Sing" at the 1938 Benny Goodman Carnegie Hall concert is considered a masterpiece of imaginative, spontaneous improvisation and was hailed by some observers as the highlight of the evening.

Artie Shapiro, bass; Joe Marsala (left foreground); Eddie Condon, guitar; Jess Stacy; and George Wettling.

The Recording Scene

A 1950 Decca session produced by Milt Gabler, with Cutty Cutshall, trombone; Eddie Condon, guitar; Wild Bill Davison, cornet; Peanuts Hucko, clarinet; Gene Schroeder, piano; Jack Lesberg, bass; and Buzzy Drootin, drums. Milt Gabler stands in the doorway at rear.

On the same date Ralph Sutton, two years into his eight-year run as intermission pianist at Eddie Condon's, was on hand for several solo numbers. Producer Milt Gabler, with his characteristic cigar, looks on.

The Original Dixieland Jazz Band (ODJB), which came north from New Orleans in 1916, first to Chicago and then to New York, in 1917 made the first jazz recordings. An inspiration to Bix Beiderbecke, Red Nichols, Wild Bill Davison, and others, the ODJB had enormous appeal for the young and restless and in 1919 toured England. Disbanding in the mid-1920s, the band re-formed in 1936 for several years, appearing in a *March of Time Film*, doing guest appearances on radio, and touring some of the vaudeville circuit.

This publicity photo from April 16, 1937, was perhaps for Victor, for whom the ODJB resumed recording at this time. Bass player Harry Barth (who did not record with the band) has been added here to the intact 1919 quintet of Tony Spargo (originally Sbarbaro), drums and kazoo; Larry Shields, clarinet; Eddie Edwards, trombone; leader Nick LaRocca, cornet; and J. Russel Robinson, piano.

This September 14, 1939, scene in the Victor recording studios represents another comeback, although not a successful one in career terms. Except for his monumental 1938 privately recorded Library of Congress series of reminiscences at the keyboard, the legendary pianist, bandleader, composer, arranger, and raconteur Jelly Roll Morton, whom critic Martin Williams cited as the jazz idiom's "first master of form," had not recorded for nearly a decade.

Despite friction among several of the participants, some splendid music came out of this session, organized by record shop owner Stephen Smith and presided over by the legendary Jelly Roll himself. Here he is clearly and joyfully, albeit very briefly, back in his element. However, a little more than a year after this session, Jelly left for Los Angeles, driving his Lincoln and towing his Cadillac. He was suffering from heart problems, asthma, and lingering trauma from knife wounds in the head and chest that he had received during an argument about music one evening in 1938 at the Jungle Inn, the U Street nightclub in Washington, D.C., that he had managed for a few years. He died in Los Angeles on July 10, 1941, three months before his fifty-first birthday.

Incidentally, the presence of Charles Peterson at this historic session was inadvertent. Apparently on another errand, he was without a camera and simply wandered into the studio, unaware that Jelly Roll Morton was recording on that date. With no time to return to his apartment for equipment,

he somehow managed to borrow a twin lens reflex that had but one unexposed frame on its roll. "Pete had always admired Jelly Roll," the photographer's son Don observes, "and it was a great disappointment to him that he didn't have the camera or the film stock with him to do the session justice. He would always regret that he was unable to do an entire series of candid shots of the great New Orleans pianist at work."[2]

From the left: Claude Jones (mostly off camera), trombone; Sidney Bechet, soprano saxophone; Sidney de Paris, trumpet; Zutty Singleton, drums; Albert Nicholas, clarinet; Jelly Roll Morton, piano; Happy Caldwell, tenor saxophone; and Lawrence Lucie, guitar. Not shown is bassist Wellman Braud.

The Recording Scene

The versatile Zutty Singleton keeping time for an HRS (Hot Record Society) session of Pee Wee Russell's Rhythmakers on August 31, 1938. To the left of Zutty is trombonist Dicky Wells and on the right are Pee Wee and Max Kaminsky. Off camera are tenor saxophonist Al Gold, pianist James P. Johnson, guitarist Freddie Green, and bassist Wellman Braud.

Don Peterson said, "This particular photo was my father's favorite among all of his 5000-plus jazz pictures. He felt that he got his flash in the optimum position—90 degrees from the camera's shooting axis—and was thus able to dramatically accentuate Zutty's intense expression."[3]

German expatriate Alfred Lion, arriving in New York in 1938, founded the Blue Note label in early 1939. Of independent U.S. jazz labels, only Commodore and HRS preceded it. For its June 8, 1939, session Lion assembled a leaderless group that was dubbed the Port of Harlem Seven.

Sidney Bechet is here recording his feature tune with rhythm section, a masterful "Summertime." Released under Bechet's name, the number brought to both the saxophonist and the label attention beyond the ordinary and even garnered a rave review by Deems Taylor in the *New York Times*.

Trumpeter Frankie Newton holds forth on a full band number. Teddy Bunn is on guitar and Big Sid Catlett (behind Newton's right shoulder), a ubiquitous presence at Blue Note sessions until the mid–1940s, on drums. Bassist Johnny Williams is behind to the right and trombonist J. C. Higginbotham is mostly off camera on the right. From the same June 8th session, as are the following two photos.

From the left: J. C. Higginbotham, trombone; Sidney Bechet, clarinet; Big Sid Catlett, drums; Teddy Bunn, guitar; Johnny Williams, bass; and Frankie Newton, trumpet. Pianist Meade Lux Lewis is off camera.

One Sidney clearly digging what another Sidney is putting down.

▲ December 15, 1940, HRS session of Jack Teagarden's Big Eight, a follow-up to a July session of Rex Stewart's Big Seven that had used some of the same personnel. Teagarden (second from right) and tenor saxophonist Ben Webster (center middle ground) were not present on the earlier date. Both sessions were organized by guitarist Brick Fleagle (foreground), a close friend of cornetist Rex Stewart (second from left) and an arranger whose work was used by Fletcher Henderson, Duke Ellington, Chick Webb, Jimmie Lunceford, and others. Barney Bigard (left foreground) is on clarinet, Dave Tough (center background) on drums, Billy Taylor (far right) on bass, and Billy Kyle (third from right in background) on piano. The tall black man in the right background is pianist Donald Lambert.

The Recording Scene

Billy Taylor takes a solo as "Big T" takes a rest.

New Orleans-born clarinetist Barney Bigard had a nearly six-decade career that had him a key member of the bands of King Oliver, Duke Ellington, Louis Armstrong, Kid Ory, Freddie Slack, and others.

Tenor saxophone giant Ben Webster's half-century in music included piano accompaniment to silent movies, work in territory bands, and associations with Bennie Moten, Fletcher Henderson, Duke Ellington, Blanche and Cab Calloway, and many others. He spent his final decade in Europe. Pianist Billy Kyle worked with Lucky Millinder, John Kirby, Louis Armstrong, and others.

Rex Stewart applies a "plumber's helper" to his cornet. Brick Fleagle is on guitar.

Rex's signature sound featured half-valve effects that lent a unique identity to his playing. He was a mainstay in the bands of Fletcher Henderson and Duke Ellington, and with McKinney's Cotton Pickers. He worked in many other situations, including Eddie Condon's club and with his own combos. In the 1960s Rex wrote on jazz for *down beat* and other periodicals and he is the author of two posthumously published books.

After the session fellow alcoholics Charles Peterson and Jack Teagarden share a bottle of Teachers Scotch in the trombonist's room at the Chesterfield Hotel near Times Square.

The Recording Scene

Harry Warnow, picking a name from the Manhattan telephone directory, became Raymond Scott when his older brother Mark became conductor of the CBS radio orchestra. Here is the six-member Raymond Scott Quintette at the CBS radio studios in October 1939.

From the left: Dave Harris, tenor saxophone; Lou Shoobe, bass; Pee Wee Erwin, trumpet mouthpiece; Johnny Williams, drums; Pete Pumiglio, clarinet; and Raymond Scott, piano. Overseeing the production from the control room are, presumably, the engineers.

"The Quintet [sic] . . . played some very unusual music, most of it composed by Raymond Scott," recalled Erwin. "It was highly descriptive of situations and experiences, or fantasies, and really did project musical pictures. . . . Typical titles included 'Powerhouse,' sounds made to represent a power plant or generators; 'The Toy Trumpet,' a rhythmic impression of a Christmas toy; 'Bumpy Weather Over Newark,' a rough airplane ride; 'Dinner Music for a Pack of Hungry Cannibals,' a tone poem filled for some reason with duck quacks." Pee Wee remembered Scott calling a "quack rehearsal" one afternoon. It was Pee Wee's trumpet—or perhaps its mouthpiece—that was responsible for the duck imitations.[4]

Jazz-influenced gospel singer Sister Rosetta Tharpe recording—probably at the Decca studios—in 1941. Her mother holds Rosetta's guitar.

In 1948 saxophonist and clarinetist Bob Wilber, then twenty years old and fresh from a year's tutelage by Sidney Bechet, took his own sextet into Boston's Savoy Café for a long residency. In June of 1949 this band, with Bechet as guest artist, recorded for Rudi Blesh's Circle label. From the left: Jimmy Archey, trombone; Henry Goodwin, trumpet; Wilber and Bechet, soprano saxophones; the "Duke of Iron," doing a calypso vocal; and Blesh.

Henry Goodwin looks on as mentor and disciple offer a duet on clarinets.

Of his experience as an eighteen-year-old, live-in student of Bechet in 1946 and 1947, Wilber said, "Bechet was a great teacher. I have always felt it was a great pity that he and other great jazzmen of his era didn't have the opportunity to do more teaching; they had so much to give and to pass on. I firmly believe that there is no better way of learning than apprenticeship to a master. . . . I was totally absorbed in the man and in his music. Every single day with him taught me more about music than a full year at Eastman could ever have done. The emphasis was always on the importance of communication, the telling of a story. Watching him, listening to him and playing alongside him was a constant revelation. Although I was immature in many ways, I realized at the time how privileged I was."[5]

A year and several months after their July 1949 wedding Duane and Helen Decker hosted another jazz gathering. According to Charles Peterson's typed note of many years after the fact and attached to the back of a print of this November 29, 1950, photo, "Johnny Mercer sings, accompanied by Willie Smith, at farewell party for the 'Lion' before sailing for London Concert tour." The facts are that the Lion left by air for a tour of France and North Africa, December 20, 1949, through February 7, 1950. There is no reference in his autobiography to a 1950 London visit.

From the left: Jane Smith, wife of the pianist; Helen "Daisy" Decker; lyricist, singer, and Capitol Records founder Johnny Mercer; and Willie the Lion Smith.

The party appears to have taken place in a recording studio and indeed the Lion did a session sometime in December of this year for Commodore at the urging of Milt Gabler associate Jack

Crystal (comedian Billy Crystal's father). The date inscribed on the print—as well as the other notations by Peterson—conflicts with that of the documented Commodore recording session and is evidently the result of faulty recordkeeping by the photographer.

In the 1930s, radio, by then a major entertainment medium, was bringing the sounds of big band jazz to tens of millions of households. While studio broadcasts of jazz groups had commenced in the early 1920s, on-location "remotes" from restaurants and dance halls did not occur until later in the decade. Pianist and bandleader Jaki Byard recalled that in the mid-1930s he was "tuning in on the radio to the broadcasts of the big bands from hotels, 11:30 P.M. to 2 A.M.—Ellington, Basie, Fatha Hines, Jimmie Lunceford, Benny Carter."[1]

This photo was Charles Peterson's conception of a typical swing fan. It was one of twenty or thirty poses the photographer shot of this young man, probably a model. The photo ran twice, in 1938 and 1939, as a Life magazine "Picture of the Week." Note the pork-pie hat (Lester Young's signature headgear), the record store shopping bag on the arm of the chair, and the photos by Peterson on the wall above the console radio. The stack of yachting magazines confirms that the shoot took place in the Peterson apartment.

CHAPTER **6**

The Big Bands

The Big Band Era has traditionally been assigned to the years 1935–45, more or less, but it must be clarified that this merely constitutes the period during which the genre became the nation's popular music. For before the 1920s had ended, the bands of Fletcher Henderson, Duke Ellington, Bennie Moten, Ben Pollack, Luis Russell, Andy Kirk, Earl Hines, and Louis Armstrong, McKinney's Cotton Pickers, and the bands managed by Jean Goldkette were units of ten or twelve musicians.

The big band has played an undisputed major role in jazz from the earliest years of the idiom's history to the 1990s. Indeed, no period of the music's development has been without its large ensembles; consider the turn-of-the-century New Orleans brass bands, the theater orchestras of 1920s Chicago, the Southwest territory dance bands of the 1930s, the big bands of the Swing Era, the bebop big bands of Dizzy Gillespie and Woody Herman in the 1940s and 1950s, and the large free-form units that have existed since the 1960s.

The great Fletcher Henderson, whose 1920s and early 1930s bands largely laid the foundation of the Swing Era. Arrangements by Fletcher and his brother Horace, as well as many by Don Redman, served as models for subsequent arrangers. In fact, Benny Goodman purchased a number of them for his own use. In Henderson's bands were some of the great soloists of jazz, including trumpeters Louis Armstrong, Joe Smith and Tommy Ladnier, cornetist Rex Stewart, tenor saxophonist Coleman Hawkins, and trombonist Jimmy Harrison. In the early and mid-1920s, Henderson led Ethel Waters' backup group on tour, recorded with Bessie Smith, and was house pianist for several recording companies.

This photo and the two that follow were taken on February 27, 1941, at the Roseland Ballroom, at Broadway and West 51st, scene of some of the band's earlier triumphs. The occasion celebrated Henderson's "17th Anniversary on Broadway" and cited him as the "King of Arrangers."

Jimmy Dorsey is at the mike presenting the *down beat* "Band of the Year Award" to Fletcher Henderson.

From top left: bassist Ted Sturgis, drummer Kaiser Marshall, and trumpeters Herbert Lee "Peanuts" Holland, Russell "Pops" Smith, Jonah Jones, and Bobby Williams. From the bottom left: Fletcher Henderson, saxophonists George Irish, Rudy Powell, George Dorsey, and Fred Mitchell, and trombonists Fernando Arbello and Fred Robinson.

Duke Ellington's extraordinary half-century-long career as pianist, composer, and leader of a band filled with many of the great musicians of jazz continued into 1974, the year he died at age seventy-five. Duke thought of the orchestra as his instrument and it truly was, for he built his pieces around the personal instrumental and vocal sounds of his players and singers. Although nearly constantly on the road for most of his adult life, Ellington composed several thousand tunes, many of which have become standards of the jazz repertoire. He wrote in large forms as well, including suites, film and musical comedy scores, liturgical music, and an uncompleted opera. To borrow a phrase he used of those whom he especially admired, Duke was "beyond category."

Pictured with him here at an August 1939 private party and jam session organized for a *Life* article (which never appeared in the magazine) are Ivie Anderson, Ellington band vocalist from 1931–42; singer and showman Cab Calloway (far right), who fronted big bands from the late 1920s into the early 1950s and sporadically thereafter into the 1990s; record producer Harry Lim (to the right of Duke); trumpeter Max Kaminsky (whose face is partly obscured by Duke's right shoulder); and trombonist J. C. Higginbotham (behind Ivie and Lim). A guest, the French jazz fan, looks on from behind Max.

Louis Armstrong at the Paramount Theatre on Broadway in May 1937. The theater, which also booked movies and stage shows, had by this time become one of the principal New York venues for big bands, white and black.

A thirty-six-year-old "Pops" enjoying a sip of beer and a bite between sets of the Paramount engagement.

At Harlem's Apollo Theatre in February 1942. The great trumpet player and singer would continue leading a big band until the summer of 1947 when he formed the six-man All Stars, which remained his format until his death in 1971. From the left: Henderson Chambers, Norman Green, George Washington (behind Armstrong), trombones; Frank Galbreath (behind Washington), Gene Prince, Shelton "Scad" Hemphill, trumpets; Joe Garland, Rupert Cole, Carl B. Frye, saxophones; Big Sid Catlett (behind Frye), drums. Saxophonist Prince Robinson, guitarist Lawrence Lucie, bassist Hayes Alvis, and pianist Luis Russell are off camera.

Multi-instrumentalist (trombone, guitar, flute, and all the saxophones) Jimmie Lunceford usually conducted, rather than played with, his widely touring band, one of the most popular big bands from the mid-1930s until its ranks were seriously depleted a year or so into World War II. Big band historian Leo Walker, who promoted one-nighters in Oregon in the late 1930s and early 1940s, recalls that in 1940 he "was offered the band for a February one-nighter at $500 . . . which was considered good money then, and on a level with most other top-rated bands who played the Pacific Northwest at that time."[2] Jimmie Lunceford was stricken with a fatal heart attack while on tour in that area in 1947. He was forty-five.

With Lunceford here at the Kit Kat Club on October 20, 1938, is alto saxophonist Willie Smith, a member of the band for most of its history and subsequently a featured soloist with many other big bands, including those of Harry James, Duke Ellington, and Billy May, and in the 1940s and 1950s with Norman Granz's Jazz at the Philharmonic. In the left foreground is French jazz critic Hugues Panassié.

In 1933 saxophonist Charlie Barnet began a two-decade career as a bandleader, continuing after that to occasionally form big bands into the mid-1960s. Barnet was—along with Benny Goodman, Artie Shaw, Eddie Condon, Art Hodes, Mezz Mezzrow, Wild Bill Davison, and a number of other white jazz musicians of the 1930s and 1940s—a pioneer integrationist. Beginning in the mid-1930s, Barnet hired Roy Eldridge, Ram Ramirez, Benny Carter, Frankie Newton, Dizzy Gillespie, Clark Terry, and many other black musicians.

Here Charlie is in residence at The Famous Door in February 1939. From the left: Kurt Bloom, tenor saxophone; Don Ruppersburg, trombone; Johnny Mendel, trumpet; Don Mc-Cook, alto; Bill Robertson (behind McCook), trombone; Charlie Huffine (background), trumpet; Barnet. To the right of Barnet are trumpeter Bobby Burnet (behind Barnet's shoulder); tenor and baritone saxophonist Jimmy Lamare (foreground), brother of guitarist Nappy Lamare; guitarist Bus Etri; drummer Wesley Dean (above Etri); pianist Nat Jaffe (far right foreground); and bassist Phil Stevens (standing above Jaffe). Trombonist Ben Hall and altoist Gene Kinsey, members of the band at this time, are presumably present but hidden by Barnet. The "Band of the Week" banner likely indicates the Monday night filler for the Barnet band's night off.

BENNY GOODMAN

Benny Goodman had already led pickup bands for college proms, a Broadway musical pit band, a backup band for singer Russ Columbo, and studio recording combos when he organized his first regularly performing big band for an engagement in Billy Rose's Music Hall at Broadway and 53rd Street. Hired at union scale—$850 a week—the band opened on June 21, 1934, and stayed for four months.

The next big break for Goodman came later that fall when his band was chosen as the "hot" band that would alternate nightly with a Latin band and a "sweet" band on NBC's new "Let's Dance" program. The late-night broadcasts from New York of the by then well warmed-up Benny Goodman band aired for two hours beginning at 9:30 P.M. in California and helped create a large youthful following. This half-year of prime-time exposure, along with good West Coast sales of the band's records and much air play, accounted for the mob scene greeting the orchestra at L.A.'s Palomar Ballroom on August 21, 1935, an historic occasion that symbolically kicked off the Swing Era. "There was wall-to-wall people," recalled the band's singer Helen Ward. "It was . . . just fantastic! And Benny's attitude was . . . , 'Well . . . , let's do the killerdillers first.' Well, that's when the crowds went crazy! The place . . . was about a block square . . . and the people just stood around the bandstand . . . and screamed. . . . The scene was just unforgettable."[3] Also with the band were Bunny Berigan, Jess Stacy, and Gene Krupa.

Benny and band play to dancers here in the Waldorf Astoria's Empire Room on New Year's Eve, 1938, only a few days before the end of a ten-week residency. Tenor saxophonist, clarinetist, and flute player Jerry Jerome has his back to the camera in the left foreground. Following are two more scenes from the same shoot.

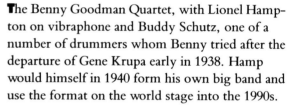

The Benny Goodman Quartet, with Lionel Hampton on vibraphone and Buddy Schutz, one of a number of drummers whom Benny tried after the departure of Gene Krupa early in 1938. Hamp would himself in 1940 form his own big band and use the format on the world stage into the 1990s.

Pianist Teddy Wilson, who led his own big band from May 1939 until the spring of 1940, is shown here soloing, closely watched by admirers.

Goodman band members Johnny Guarnieri and singer Helen Forrest rehearsing in 1941. Helen joined the Goodman band, at half the weekly $175 Artie Shaw had been paying her, in December 1939, a few weeks after Artie impulsively walked off the bandstand one night and moved to Mexico for several months. She left Goodman three months after this photo was taken and went with Harry James for two years. One of the most popular big band singers of the era, Helen Forrest continued to perform into the 1980s. Guarnieri also worked with Shaw, as well as with Jimmy Dorsey, Raymond Scott, and others. Johnny reinforced his popularity through ubiquitous appearances on 52nd Street and on many recordings during the 1940s.

THE DORSEY BROTHERS

As leaders of the Dorsey Brothers Orchestra, Tommy and Jimmy Dorsey had been recording since 1928. It was in the spring of 1934 that they first organized a band for regular in-person performances. The collaboration, threatened from the start by sibling rivalry that sometimes erupted in fist fights on the bandstand, survived only into the summer of 1935, when Tommy walked out and established his own band.

More than three hundred musicians passed through the bands of Tommy and Jimmy Dorsey in the two decades they were active as leaders. Among the several dozen who served with the Dorseys as instrumentalists, vocalists, or arrangers and who would subsequently become bandleaders or headliners themselves were Bing Crosby, the Boswell Sisters, Glenn Miller, Bud Freeman, Dave Tough, Bunny Berigan, Charlie Teagarden, Sy Oliver, Buddy Rich, Frank Sinatra, Don Redman, Gene Krupa, Charlie Shavers, Louie Bellson, Terry Gibbs, and Doc Severinsen.

Tommy is here pictured in 1936 with his vocalists, Jack Leonard and Edythe Wright.

Many of the name bands carried a "band-within-a-band," a more compact unit suitable for interludes of a looser nature than the big band format allowed. Tommy Dorsey's Clambake Seven is seen here at another one of those photo-opportunity-arranged jam sessions, this time backstage at the Paramount Theatre, where the Tommy Dorsey Orchestra was performing on October 20, 1938. From the left: Yank Lawson, trumpet; Howard Smith, piano; Carmen Mastren, guitar; French

jazz critic Hugues Panassié (foreground) and Johnny Mince, clarinets; Panassié's colleague Madeleine Gautier; Gene Traxler, bass; Tommy, trombone; Maurice "Moe" Purtill, drums; and Skeets Herfurt, tenor saxophone.

The movie poster on the back wall represents the 1938 "If I Were King," a Paramount Studios production starring Ronald Colman and Frances Dee. It was perhaps the very film the Dorsey orchestra was sharing the bill with.

Multi-instrumentalist (alto saxophone, clarinet, and, briefly in the 1920s, trumpet) and bandleader Jimmy Dorsey on alto. The trombonists are, from the left, Sonny Lee, Bobby Byrne, and Don Matteson. March 9, 1938, location unknown.

Fronted by Bing Crosby's younger brother, who was also a singer, the fine Bob Crosby band came together in 1935 and broke up in 1942. Scaled down for Dixieland selections into an eight-member band-within-a-band, the Bob Cats featured regular members New Orleans native Ray Bauduc on drums and Bob Haggart on bass. On this March 1940 date Charles Peterson shot the Crosby big band, the Bob Cats, and several other groups performing at the New Yorker Hotel for *Life* magazine.

On the same date, trumpeter Billy Butterfield, who also served in the bands of Artie Shaw, Benny Goodman, and Les Brown, takes a solo with the full Crosby band. The trumpeter between Bauduc and Billy is Max Herman.

A major figure of the big band era and a clarinet virtuoso, Artie Shaw led a band from 1936 for the better part of two decades with many interruptions, including a year and a half of duty as a Navy bandleader in the South Pacific during World War II. In 1954 he left music altogether to become a writer. From the left: Chuck Peterson (far left and no relation to the photographer) and Bernie Privin, trumpets; Tony Pastor (foreground), tenor saxophone; and George Arus (beneath Artie's arm), trombone. To the right is drummer George Wettling. Blue Room, Hotel Lincoln, December 1938.

In terms of years as a big-band leader in jazz, only Duke Ellington matched Woody Herman's longevity and only Lionel Hampton and Les Brown have surpassed him. In 1986, the year before his death, Woody celebrated his fiftieth anniversary at the helm of his band. At the microphone here in 1939, he seems to be delivering a vocal. From the left: Saxie Mansfield, tenor saxophone; Joe Bishop (behind Mansfield), flugelhorn; Joe Estren, alto; Steady Nelson and Clarence Willard (with mute in horn), trumpets. Behind Woody is trombonist Neil Reid and above his left shoulder is flutist (and baritonist) Roy Hopfner. Drummer Frank Carlson is in the right background and pianist Tommy Linehan is off-camera to the left.

The presence of French jazz critic Hugues Panassié establishes this scene as having taken place in the Victor recording studios on October 20, 1938, the date on which trumpeter Erskine Hawkins and His Orchestra, a fourteen-member unit plus two singers, recorded six 78 rpm sides for Bluebird. On camera, from the left, are guitarist William McLemore, alto saxophonist Jimmy Mitchelle, baritonist and clarinetist Haywood Henry, bassist Leemie Stanfield, Panassié, Hawkins, and tenorist Julian Dash. Hawkins, who was billed as "The Twentieth Century Gabriel," was active from the mid–1930s well into the 1950s as leader of a blues-oriented dance band that featured fine soloists and was popular with black audiences.

Red Norvo, who had been featured on xylophone earlier with the Paul Whiteman orchestra, led big bands from the mid-1930s to the mid-1940s. His musical approach was progressive for the time and he hired top players like Remo Palmieri and Eddie Bert, as well as master arranger Eddie Sauter.

Here he is during a March 1938 reengagement at the Commodore Hotel with Mildred Bailey, generally ranked as the premier white jazz vocalist of the era. Norvo and Bailey, "Mr. and Mrs. Swing," were married from 1933 until 1945. From the left: Len Goldstein, Hank D'Amico, alto saxophones; Jerry Jerome (behind Mildred), tenor; Wes Hein, Barney Zudecoff, Zeke Zarchy, Jimmy Blair, trumpets; George Wettling, drums.

Charles Peterson shot this 1938 publicity photo of Mildred Bailey in his New York studio several doors from the Algonquin Hotel, where prominent writers, composers, and performing artists, including Alexander Woollcott, Dorothy Parker, and George Kaufman, met daily for lunch. The photographer built the set from weatherbeaten shingles, doors, and windows, the remains of a demolished shed on the grounds of his summertime retreat near Point Pleasant, New Jersey.

This photo of Mildred saw widespread circulation. The theme was, of course, suggested by Hoagy Carmichael's "Rockin' Chair," which she recorded several times. The song remained in her repertoire so long, in fact, that in the 1930s Mildred came to be known as the "Rockin' Chair Lady."

GLENN MILLER

Glenn Miller had already worked for Ben Pollack, Red Nichols, and the Dorsey Brothers by the time he formed his own band in 1937. Distinctive arrangements, exposure via radio and Hollywood, and a string of hit records combined to earn the Glenn Miller band nationwide fame as a dance orchestra that divided its book between sentimental popular tunes and mildly swinging up-tempo numbers. It had become one of the highest paid bands in the country by the time Miller was commissioned a captain in the U.S. Army Air Force in October 1942. He was given the task of forming a service band, which initially toured the United States on recruitment drives and then, as the Glenn Miller AEF Orchestra, sailed for England in 1944. Miller's life ended in December of that year when he went to check out arrangements for an appearance in Paris and the small plane carrying him disappeared over the English Channel.

The several photos that follow were all shot at the Meadowbrook Ballroom in Cedar Grove, New Jersey, November 29, 1939. Here Miller leads his trombone section. On the left, the trumpeter in the background is Dale "Mack" McMickle and behind Glenn's shoulder is trumpeter Johnny Best. The trombonist in the left foreground is Frank D'Annolfo. On the right above Glenn's shoulder is trumpeter Clyde Hurley.

The Miller reed section. From the left: Al Klink, tenor saxophone; Wilbur Schwartz, Hal McIntyre and Jimmy Abato, altos; and Tex Beneke, tenor.

Maurice "Moe" Purtill appears to be launching one of his spectacular, crowd-pleasing drum solos. Rowland "Rolly" Bundock is on bass.

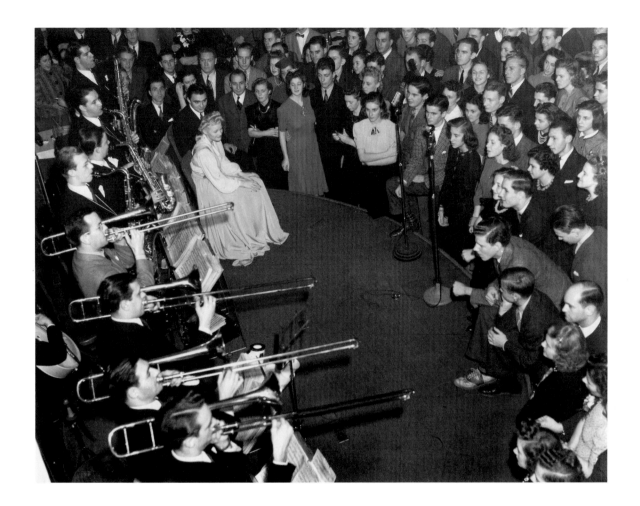

Often dancers broke ranks and just stood and dug the band. In the trombone section, from the top, are Glenn Miller, Paul Tanner, Al Mastren, and Frank D'Annolfo. The guitar in the left foreground is being played by Richard Fisher and in front of the saxophone section are band singers Marion Hutton (in white gown) and Ray Eberle (standing behind her). Not shown are pianist Chummy MacGregor and trumpeter Leigh Knowles. The saxophonists are, from the top, Tex Beneke, Jimmy Abato, Hal McIntyre, and Al Klink.

Popular bandleader Miller shares a break with some of his fans.

Whatever the Miller band is putting down at this moment, the two who command the floor definitely appear to be with it, and their audience seems transfixed by their moves.

featured shows on a rotating stage (dinner, dancing, and show at $2.00 on Saturday, $1.50 on weeknights). We see here, on April 16, 1938 (about halfway into the band's residency there), in the right foreground, tenor saxophonist Georgie Auld and altoist Joe Dixon. Trombonist Sonny Lee is above Dixon. To the left of Bunny are trumpeter Irving Goodman (foreground), brother of Benny, and drummer Johnny Blowers.

Trumpeter/trombonist Larry Clinton, who had played in or arranged for Glen Gray and the Casa Loma Orchestra and the bands of Isham Jones, the Dorseys, and Bunny Berigan, led his own big band from 1938–41 and then resumed for several years in the late 1940s. Here he rehearses his brass section in New York's Haven recording studio on January, 21, 1941. From the left: trombonists Jimmy Curry, Clinton, Miff Sines, and Howard Gibeling; and trumpeters Walter Smith, Bob Alexy, and Henry Cowan. Alto saxophonist Ben Feman is in the left foreground and baritonist Butch Stone is in the right foreground.

Trumpeter Bunny Berigan's brief career—he was a professional musician from his late teens and died at the age of thirty-three—included associations with the Dorseys, Paul Whiteman, and Benny Goodman; combo leadership; studio work; and five years (1937–42) on the road with his musically vital but often financially troubled big band.

Bunny's was the first jazz band to be booked into the prestigious Paradise Restaurant, which

Gene Krupa formed his first big band upon leaving Benny Goodman in early 1938 and continued to lead it (with approximately a year's interruption caused by legal difficulties in 1943) into the mid-1950s. This photo is from the Carnegie Hall Fats Waller concert of January 14, 1942, at which time Gene's band was breaking house records at the Paramount Theatre.

Having several years earlier led a college band at Duke University, Les Brown in 1938 formed his soon-to-be extremely popular "Band of Renown," essentially a dance unit but one that over the years usually included several jazz players—for example, trumpeter Billy Butterfield, drummer Shelley Manne, and Abe Most. The band performed nationwide for a decade, after which Brown commenced a long association with Bob Hope as musical director for his radio and television shows.

Brown (standing), on alto saxophone, was caught here in a May 22, 1941, recording session rehearsal. The singer is Betty Bonney and the trumpeters on the date were Robert Thorne, Eddie Bailey, and Joe Bogart, two of whom can be seen in the background. The others are, from the left: bassist Charlie Green; drummer Eddie Julian; baritone saxophonist Eddie Sheer; trombonist Warren Brown (behind mike stand); Bonney, altoist Abe Most; trombonists Zi Zentner and Ronnie Chase; altoist Steve Madrick; and tenorist Wolfe Tayne (only his leg is visible at far right). Guitarist Joe Petroni and pianist William Rowland are off camera.

Harry James, a star of the Goodman band for almost two years, put together a big band in early 1939 and remained its leader until ten days before his death in 1983.

"My dad started to teach me trumpet when I was nine," Harry said a half year or so before he died, "and by the time I was eleven I was playing in the circus band with him. My idol at all times was Louis Armstrong. As far as I was concerned, there wasn't anyone but him."[4]

With Harry here at, probably, the Pennsylvania Hotel (Charles Peterson's note says "Philadelphia Hotel") in March or April 1939 are alto saxophonist Dave Matthews (left foreground) and tenorist Claude Lakey. Trombonist Truett Jones is in the left background and the guitar on the right is Bryan "Red" Kent's.

Tenor saxophonist and singer Tony Pastor left Artie Shaw the year before he started his own big band in 1940. He kept it together until the late 1950s. This photo captures him during a characteristically good-humored vocal at the Lincoln Hotel on February 25, 1941. At far left is tenor saxophonist Robert Taylor and to the right of the microphone stand is probably trombonist Bill Abel.

JACK TEAGARDEN

After five years as a featured jazz soloist with Paul Whiteman, trombone master Jack Teagarden had had enough of "symphonic jazz" and in early 1939 put together his first big band. By virtue of his own enormous talents and top sidemen the likes of his brother Charlie, Lee Castle, and Charlie Spivak on trumpets, baritone saxophonist and clarinetist Ernie Caceres, and drummer Dave Tough, this first band earned high marks for its sounds but teetered on the brink of financial disaster, finally falling in after a year and leaving its leader nearly $50,000 in the hole. Forming another band, Mr. T kept it together until 1946 when he left the business side of big bands for good. The next year he joined Louis Armstrong's All Stars, staying with Satchmo until 1951 and thereafter heading his own combos.

Younger brother Charlie Teagarden also led a big band briefly in the early 1940s. With him in this April 19, 1941, photo is accordionist Joe Mooney, a featured guest with Charlie's band on this occasion.

Here in rehearsal in January 1939 are some members of Jack's initial sixteen-member unit. From the left: "Big T"; Ernie Caceres, baritone saxophone; Art Miller, bass; Allen Reuss, guitar; Max Kaminsky, trumpet; Jack's younger brother Clois "Cubby" Teagarden, drums; and Clint Garvin, clarinet.

As a member of the Paul Whiteman Orchestra, Jack Teagarden, decked out in bandsman's attire, was the featured player in the circus band numbers of the 1935 Billy Rose musical extravaganza *Jumbo*. Richard Rodgers and Lorenz Hart wrote the score, Ben Hecht the book, and comedian Jimmy Durante starred. The show is considered a great musical production but was so expensive to stage that it never made money, despite a half-year or so run on Broadway at the Hippodrome. This late 1935 photo, from one of Charles Peterson's earliest shoots, originally appeared with a half-dozen others by him in a 1936 issue of *Town and Country*, accompanying an article by novelist Frank Norris on swing.

NOTES

CHAPTER 1
Harlem

1. Duke Ellington, "The Most Essential Instrument," *Jazz Journal* (London), December 1965, 14–15.
2. Details on the Harlem Renaissance can be found in: Jervis Anderson, *This Was Harlem: 1900–1950* (New York: Farrar Straus Giroux, 1982); David Levering Lewis, *When Harlem Was in Vogue* (New York: Alfred A. Knopf, 1981); Bruce Kellner, ed., *The Harlem Renaissance: A Historical Dictionary for the Era* (New York: Methuen, 1987); Samuel A. Floyd, Jr., ed., *Black Music in the Harlem Renaissance: A Collection of Essays* (New York: Greenwood Press, 1990).
3. W. Royal Stokes, *The Jazz Scene: An Informal History from New Orleans to 1990* (New York: Oxford University Press, 1991), 49.
4. John Hammond (with Irving Townsend), *On Record: An Autobiography* (New York: Ridge Press/Summit Books, 1977), 206–210.
5. Count Basie, *Good Morning Blues: The Autobiography of Count Basie, As Told to Albert Murray* (New York: Random House, 1985), 69.
6. Mezz Mezzrow and Bernard Wolfe, *Really the Blues* (New York: Citadel Underground, 1990), passim.
7. Stokes, *The Jazz Scene,* 61.
8. Ibid., 163.
9. Edward Kennedy Ellington, *Music Is My Mistress* (New York: Doubleday & Co., Inc., 1973), 124.
10. Stokes, *The Jazz Scene,* 67–68. For some riveting descriptions of the early 1940s dance scene in the Savoy and in Boston's Roseland State Ballroom, see, respectively, Chapters 5 and 3 of *The Autobiography of Malcolm X* (with the assistance of Alex Haley) (New York: Grove Press, 1966).
11. Stokes, *The Jazz Scene,* 53–54.
12. Willie the Lion Smith with George Hoefer, *Music on My Mind: The Memoirs of an American Pianist* (New York: Doubleday & Co., 1964), 155.
13. Stokes, *The Jazz Scene,* 60.
14. Smith, *Music on My Mind,* 155.

CHAPTER 2
52nd Street

1. Note to the author, 1993.
2. Stokes, *The Jazz Scene,* 58.
3. Ibid., 58.

CHAPTER 3
Nick's, the Village Vanguard, Café Society, and Other Venues

1. Bud Freeman, *You Don't Look Like a Musician* (Detroit: Balamp Publishing, 1974), 6–7.

2. Dizzy Gillespie with Al Fraser, *To Be or Not to Bop: Memoirs* (New York: Doubleday & Co., 1979), 153.
3. Whitney Balliett, *Barney, Bradley, and Max: Sixteen Portraits in Jazz* (New York: Oxford University Press, 1989), 44.
4. From a 1950 interview conducted by Leonard Feather and included in Lewis Porter, ed., *A Lester Young Reader* (Washington, D.C.: Smithsonian Institution Press, 1991), 145.
5. Buck Clayton, assisted by Nancy Miller Elliott, *Buck Clayton's Jazz World* (New York: Oxford University Press, 1987), 144.
6. Related by Bill Goodall to Don Peterson, 1992.
7. Artie Shaw, *The Trouble With Cinderella: An Outline Of Identity* (New York: Da Capo Press, 1979), 293.
8. Robert Dupuis, *Bunny Berigan: Elusive Legend Of Jazz* (Baton Rouge: Louisiana State University Press, 1993), 111, citing Helen Oakley's review in *down beat*, August 1, 1935.
9. Stokes, *The Jazz Scene*, 91.

CHAPTER 4

Jam Sessions

1. Donald M. Marquis, *In Search of Buddy Bolden: First Man of Jazz* (Baton Rouge: Louisiana State University Press, 1978), 81 ff.
2. Stokes, *The Jazz Scene,* 154.
3. Ibid., 19–21 and 25–27; also, cf. William Howland Kenney, *Chicago Jazz: A Cultural History, 1904–1930* (New York: Oxford University Press, 1993), 114–15 and 165.
4. Stokes, *The Jazz Scene,* 40–42.
5. Ibid., 53–54 and 59–60.
6. Ibid., 62.

7. Ibid., 211.
8. Ibid., 133–34 and 137–38.
9. Ibid., 143–45
10. Ibid., 241–42.
11. Max Kaminsky and V. E. Hughes, *Jazz Band: My Life in Jazz* (New York: Da Capo Press, 1981), 122–23.
12. Stokes, *The Jazz Scene*, 21.
13. Eddie Condon (with Thomas Sugrue), *We Called It Music: A Generation of Jazz* (New York: Da Capo Press, 1992), 266.

CHAPTER 5

The Recording Scene

1. Condon, *We Called It Music*, 264.
2. Note to the author.
3. Note to the author.
4. Pee Wee Erwin (as told to Warren W. Vaché, Sr.), *This Horn for Hire* (Metuchen, N.J.: The Scarecrow Press and the Institute of Jazz Studies of Rutgers University, 1987), 180.
5. Bob Wilber (assisted by Derek Webster), *Music Was Not Enough* (New York: Oxford University Press, 1988), 25 and 29.

CHAPTER 6

The Big Bands

1. Stokes, *The Jazz Scene,* 98.
2. Leo Walker, *The Big Band Almanac*, revised edition (New York: Da Capo Press, 1989), 269.
3. Stokes, *The Jazz Scene,* 69–70.
4. Ibid., 89.

INDEX OF PICTURED SUBJECTS

217